S0-AYG-319

WITHDRAWN

BUILD
FOR
CHANGE

ALAN TREFLER

BUILD FOR CHANGE

REVOLUTIONIZING

CUSTOMER ENGAGEMENT THROUGH

CONTINUOUS DIGITAL INNOVATION

WILEY

Cover image and design: Wiley

Copyright © 2014 by Pegasystems, Inc. All rights reserved.

Published by John Wiley & Sons, Inc., Hoboken, New Jersey.
Published simultaneously in Canada.

No part of this publication may be reproduced, stored in a retrieval system, or transmitted
in any form or by any means, electronic, mechanical, photocopying, recording, scanning,
or otherwise, except as permitted under Section 107 or 108 of the 1976 United States
Copyright Act, without either the prior written permission of the Publisher, or authorization
through payment of the appropriate per-copy fee to the Copyright Clearance Center, 222
Rosewood Drive, Danvers, MA 01923, (978) 750-8400, fax (978) 646-8600, or on the web
at www.copyright.com. Requests to the Publisher for permission should be addressed to the
Permissions Department, John Wiley & Sons, Inc., 111 River Street, Hoboken, NJ 07030,
(201) 748-6011, fax (201) 748-6008, or online at www.wiley.com/go/permissions.

Limit of Liability/Disclaimer of Warranty: While the publisher and author have used their
best efforts in preparing this book, they make no representations or warranties with the
respect to the accuracy or completeness of the contents of this book and specifically disclaim
any implied warranties of merchantability or fitness for a particular purpose. No warranty
may be created or extended by sales representatives or written sales materials. The advice
and strategies contained herein may not be suitable for your situation. You should consult
with a professional where appropriate. Neither the publisher nor the author shall be liable for
damages arising herefrom.

For general information about our other products and services, please contact our Customer
Care Department within the United States at (800) 762-2974, outside the United States at
(317) 572-3993 or fax (317) 572-4002.

Wiley publishes in a variety of print and electronic formats and by print-on-demand.
Some material included with standard print versions of this book may not be included in
e-books or in print-on-demand. If this book refers to media such as a CD or DVD that
is not included in the version you purchased, you may download this material at http://
booksupport.wiley.com. For more information about Wiley products, visit www.wiley.com.

ISBN: 978-1-118-93026-7 (cloth)

ISBN: 978-1-118-93028-1 (ebk)

ISBN: 978-1-118-893029-8 (ebk)

Printed in the United States of America

10 9 8 7 6 5 4 3 2 1

CONTENTS

FOREWORD

So much has changed in the business world, particularly in the past 20 years. Two changes are particularly relevant to this book. First, thanks to the ubiquity of technology and the reach of the Internet, the power of customers has reached dramatic levels. You will see many examples of this phenomenon in the pages ahead. Second, companies can now fully digitize their processes to the point where the enterprise can and must undergo a full digital transformation. It is the only way the enterprise will accomplish the seamless operations so vital to success. But as this happens, the enterprise must focus on how, through both high tech and high touch, it engages customers and responds to their expectations.

This book lays out the path to accomplishing that result.

There will be several challenges along the way. Past approaches to systems development have left companies frozen in technology, unable to respond to both opportunities and the demands of customers. Companies cannot solve this problem by simply buying apps or software as a service. Technology and process must be more tightly integrated in the work of digitization. That integration will require that the divide between the information technology (IT) and business communities goes away. As this happens, the organization itself will undergo change.

That change will include how people think of their own work: how work is performed and customers are engaged; the pace of work and the rate at which operational change can be accomplished; the ability to see how radically the performance of an enterprise can improve with the right approach to technology and process, as business and IT people come together to drive change.

Changes in thinking and behavior will not be restricted just to the workers. No great change is achieved unless an enterprise's leaders and managers change how they think and behave. What has been the key to past success may not be the key to success in the future. That is especially true with respect to the role of information technology and how it is managed.

Twenty years ago, Michael Hammer and I published *Reengineering the Corporation*. We described "the three Cs"—customers, competition, and change—as the forces driving companies into frighteningly unfamiliar territory. New entrants to markets were intensifying competition by changing the rules of business, while the pace of business change itself was accelerating. Meanwhile, customers were gaining the upper hand in their relationships with sellers, with access to more information and more choice, and were becoming increasingly sophisticated and demanding.

In some respects, what we wrote was seen as predictive. All this was happening while companies were stuck in their bureaucratic structures and fragmented work. Meanwhile, customers in particular were beginning to drive the need for change. We wrote that business customers and individual consumers "know what they want, what they want to pay for it, and how to get it on the terms they demand." We warned that "customers such as these don't need to deal with companies that don't understand and appreciate this startling change in the customer-seller relationship." Customers will just go elsewhere.

Today, customers are doing just that.

We argued for radical change in the nature of work, with a focus on the redesign of business processes. Today, the phenomena we described are plain to see, and drive the urgency of what you will read in this book.

The cry for leaders and managers to wake up to the changing business landscape and the importance and power of technology is not new. I have made the plea and have heard it for years. But what is new is the approach to the digitization of the enterprise that this book lays out. Time is of the essence. While customers have been gaining power, the pace of business change is also accelerating. It is time to think radically about how technology plays and works in your enterprise.

—James Champy
Coauthor of *Reengineering the Corporation*;
Author of *X-Engineering the Corporation:*
Reinventing Your Business in the Digital Age

ACKNOWLEDGMENTS

This book is the product of decades of engagement with many of the world's most sophisticated organizations. I would like to thank the clients who have shared their views on the imminent threats, as well as their managerial and technological responses. Their journeys are the real story of this book, and it has been a privilege to see firsthand how insight and innovation can lead to differentiated success.

Capturing and refining these ideas has been a journey in itself. Let me thank the team of Brian Callahan, Scott Cooper, and Russell Keziere for invaluable assistance in getting to this point.

Thanks also to the Central Square Theater (www.centralsquare theater.org) for organizing the focus group quoted in this book. This included cast members, aged 14 to 22, of *Six Years Online* by Betsy Bard, a play that explores how social media shapes day-to-day communication.

The work behind this book continues—both with clients and in the creation of technology that empowers new approaches to customer engagement. Comments are welcomed at alan.trefler@pega.com.

Cambridge, Massachusetts

1

CUSTOMERPOCALYPSE

A lot of companies across the globe are going to die over the next few years, not because of macroeconomic stress but because there is an entire emerging generation of customers who hate doing business with them. These companies are going to die from some form of *customer stress*. Death may come as the result of self-inflicted wounds the company should have known to avoid, which means it is kind of like suicide. It may come from involuntary manslaughter by a new generation of customers. Or these new kinds of customers may just outright murder companies they decide should be put out of their misery. It is the *customerpocalypse*.

Who are these customers? They trace their ancestry first to the Millennials, also known as Generation Y. The latter term comes from an editorial in *Ad Age* in 1993, which attempted to describe the teenagers of that time and how they differed from Generation X, the name given to the generation born after the post-World War II baby boom popularized by the novelist Douglas Coupland.[1] When *Ad Age* coined the Gen Y term, it applied to kids 12 and younger at the time, and was meant to refer to those kids who would become teenagers over the subsequent 10 years.

The Millennials term is widely credited to William Strauss and Neil Howe from work first published in 1991.[2] You may also have heard of them referred to as Generation We, Generation Next, and the Net Generation. They account for about 75 million people in the United States alone. The generation's earliest days are just around the time digital technologies for the general public first appeared, beginning with Apple's first personal computer, the IBM PC, and Microsoft's early PC operating system. They grew up with digital technology, and came of age as it, too, came of age, beginning its slow, steady march to ubiquity. Over the course of their lives, digital technology has become a commodity, fundamentally changing what they expect and how they interact. Millennials are also the generation that grew up with play dates and adolescent team sports that awarded everyone a trophy for playing in the soccer game, whether they won or lost. This "ethic" figures into how they view the world and the relationships they have with your business as your (potential) customer.

Diane Theilfoldt and Devon Scheef aptly synopsized their characteristics in a 2004 article. Millennials are (among other things) "self-inventive/individualistic"; they "rewrite the rules"; they consider institutions irrelevant; the Internet is their world; they don't just use but "assume" technology is there for everything; and they "multitask fast."[3]

From this Millennial/Gen Y group, another name emerged: Generation C. The name works in part because, as entertaining as Douglas Coupland's declaration of Generation X was, he did us the disservice of choosing a letter far too far along in the alphabet to continue with his naming convention. More important is that unlike the Gen X and Gen Y names, Gen C includes a characterization within its very name.

"[T]he C stands for CONTENT, and anyone with even a tiny amount of creative talent can (and probably will) be a part of this not-so-exclusive trend."[4] These are the young people who are responsible for—and who revel in—all manner of content on the World Wide Web. They post and curate. They are the self-proclaimed editors of Wikipedia. They made YouTube the amazing repository of content that it is today.

Despite its relative youth, this group influences every aspect of our lives and wreaks havoc on many businesses.[5] Gen C accounts for about 75 million people in the United States alone. Still growing in size by leaps and bounds, largely now from the emergence of new economies in much of the less-developed world and changing economies in places such as Russia, China, and India, Gen C is fast becoming the largest group of consumers in the entire world.

It's important to note that the divisions between the generations discussed in this book are rather fluid. Gen C has really come into its own with the shift in the meaning of the C; it is that very shift that leads to the observation that today there is actually a Gen C-1 and a Gen C-2 coexisting in time. Members of Gen C-1, who came first and tend to be more passive, are generally older than the more active members of Gen C-2. They are the members of the Gen C segment who *publish*.

With the evolution of the mobile Web, Gen C evolved from *content* to *communicating, computerized, clicking* and, finally, *connected.* It is the advent of *connected mobility* that has given rise to Gen C-2. This component of the larger Gen C arose with the sudden democratization of communications and the unmediated access to personalized mass communication, exemplified by Twitter, but not exclusive to that technology tool. They are the ones who use on-the-spot messaging to create flash mobs and take down repressive governments as happened during the Arab Spring.

If Gen C-1 is the *publish* or *post* segment, then Gen C-2 is the *ping* part of the group. Gen C members have gone from asynchronous communication through e-mail and Facebook to always-on, always-linked interactions that are synchronous, happening in real time. Gen C-2 is even helping drive a move away from e-mail.[6] More relevant to the discussion here is that Gen C is the generation that pushed connectivity to the point where there are 10.5 billion active memberships across at least 158 online social communities—and that is exclusive of Facebook and YouTube, which add another 1 billion each.[7] Gen C is why every company has a Facebook page and a Twitter account, even if most corporate types using them have little idea, or in many cases absolutely no idea, what they are doing.

Great Expectations

As a whole, Gen C has some major expectations that create big challenges for companies. For instance, they expect to be able to engage with your Website and perhaps even talk to someone in your call center at the same time. They expect your company to be as centered on them as they are centered on themselves. If they know something, they expect you to know it, too. They do not care whether you have separate divisions to handle products or services they buy from you. In fact, if you use that as an excuse for why you had to ask a stupid question (yes, in this world there *are* many stupid questions), they will come to hate you even more.

Gen C customers have no patience when you try to sell them some lame product they would never consider in a million years.

If they have a problem, they expect you to fix it in a way that makes sense.

Fail a Gen C customer, and she may or may not tell you how she feels. The best case for your company is that she just puts up with it and keeps on with what she is already doing with your business. That particular best case is not too likely to occur. What is more likely is that she will tell all of her connected "friends" about how you failed and how she is taking her business elsewhere. The Website Yelp has been a popular online destination for members of Gen C. Maybe you have seen a post like this on Yelp:

> Tried out Super Falafel, the new place in my hood, and it hella crap. Will never go back. Surly counter help, everything lukewarm, don't take cards. Sorry to Falafel City, my old standby near work. Still great after all these years!

The post is seen by lots of other people, and online "friends" of the original poster might even get notifications when one of their friends posts. They then comment and add their own experiences—with business implications that should be obvious.

Someone among the friends and followers may even revert to his content roots and share the experience on a Website set up for no reason other than to mock your company and share the many stories of how it has failed Gen C. These kinds of Websites have proliferated thanks to Gen C. Some have called them "suck sites," as in Company X sucks, and they reflect anger based on genuine experiences.

IT IS SO EASY TO LOSE CUSTOMERS

Some businesses, such as Apple and Google, have been very tuned in and successful with Gen C customers from their beginnings. But for every success story, there are countless tales of companies really messing up with Gen C customers. They fall into one of two general categories: those who screw up but recover and those who fail to listen to their customers and die. In the category of those who met their demise, consider Circuit City. Founded in 1949, the company was the first to launch an electronics superstore. That was in the 1970s. By 2009, Circuit City had liquidated its final U.S. retail store after filing for bankruptcy and failing to find a buyer. When it went under, the company was the second-largest U.S. electronics store, after its main competitor Best Buy—which is still around today.

What killed Circuit City? Alan L. Wurtzel, son of the founder and the company's CEO from 1972 to 1986 and board vice chairman or chairman from 1986 to 2001, believes it was a failure to listen.

His successors "underestimated the change in consumer taste, the change in consumer buying patterns, and they clearly underestimated the rapid rise of Best Buy." In his 2012 book about Circuit City,[8] Wurtzel explained, "One of the lessons of the book is listen to the customer, not listen to Wall Street."[9]

How about Nokia? The Finnish giant was the world's largest vendor of mobile phones from 1998 to 2012. But in September 2013, its handset business was sold to Microsoft for $7.2 billion—a figure some analysts, such as well-known business journalist James Surowiecki, believe to be quite over the top, "since a year [later] that business might well turn out to have been worth nothing."[10] Surowiecki explains, "Nokia overestimated the strength of its brand," and even "failed to recognize that brands today aren't as resilient as they once were."

Notably, Nokia had created a device very much like the iPhone some seven years before Apple released its first version. Then, when the iPhone came out, Nokia mounted a public campaign to discredit the new product from a technological and engineering point-of-view, chastising Apple for making it impossible for customers to replace the battery and pointing out that the iPhone would be damaged if dropped from a height of five feet. Meanwhile, Apple was in the business of delighting its customers, for whom Nokia's complaints were secondary.

"The high-tech era," writes Surowiecki, "has taught people to expect constant innovation; when companies fall behind, consumers are quick to punish them."

Borders is another victim of its own screwups with Gen C customers. At one point the once-popular bookseller had more than

500 stores in the United States, but in February 2011 it filed for bankruptcy protection and began to liquidate. By September of that same year, Borders was gone. What happened? "The company made some poor decisions . . . and failed to adapt to new ways consumers shop and read books," writes Rick Newman, chief business correspondent for *U.S. News & World Report*. At a time when Amazon figured out that customers would flock to e-books and developed the Kindle device and apps to support broader adoption, Borders ignored the new technology and "clung to an outdated strategy way too long and reacted slowly as more nimble competitors took its business away."[11]

The bookstore chain once had millions of loyal customers. But, as Newman continues, "loyalty is never enough." It is a message that figures prominently as you read on.

In the category of not-quite-gone companies, there is BlackBerry. In late 2013, the company agreed to be acquired by a Canadian holding company and taken private, "a turning point for a once high-flying tech giant that played a key role in the mobile-device revolution only to be eclipsed by Apple and Google." BlackBerry's products were once ubiquitous among business users in particular. But, as *Time* magazine so aptly put it, the company "failed to anticipate that consumers— not business customers—would drive the smartphone revolution."[12]

Then there are those who messed up but recovered. A recent classic involves Netflix, a company that had actually embraced the idea of connective collaboration with customers in the ways it did business and drove the giant Blockbuster video store chain into oblivion. But in 2011, Netflix made a crucial mistake. The company was hell-bent on driving its customer base to the world of online, streaming content and reconfigured its business model. But Netflix forgot that its connected customers had their own ideas about how they wanted to do business with the company and were inclined to see anything even remotely coercive as inherently evil. They weren't about to have some company—even one they had previously loved—try to change their behavior.

Netflix rolled out a series of tone-deaf pricing policies and new limitations on its service offerings. In doing so, Netflix came close to putting itself in the very shoes it had fitted for Blockbuster.

Subscribers fled in droves. Fortunately, the company was able to learn from this serious misstep, reversed the policy, and has since gone from strength to strength to dominate the subscription video on demand (SVOD) market.

The Netflix debacle played out across social media platforms, blogs, and everywhere the new generation of connected customers post, chat, talk, kvetch, promote, and detract. The company fell victim to Gen C customers who have expectations unlike anything businesses have ever seen and had to reverse itself. By the way, if you think Websites for complaining about companies are insignificant, take a look at netflix.pissedconsumer.com or amplicate.com/hate/facebook.

To companies like Netflix, add the electric company, cellphone providers, the cable company, and any number of businesses with which Gen C interacts and that are responsible for people wanting to rip wires out of their walls, flush their phones down the toilet, or throw their televisions out the window. The last thing Gen C customers want any part of is knowing that you are making business decisions to influence their behavior. They will object, they will drop you, and they will tell their friends. That's the end of it, and you will probably never recapture any of those customers.

This truly is a matter of survival. Right now, to a lot of companies, figuring out how to deal with Gen C looks like a matter of evolving existing value propositions to recapture prosperity. Believe me, that will not last long. There is a big difference between prosperity and survival, and when the time comes that it's only about survival, it will simply be too late for a lot of companies. In the customerpocalypse, recovery from missteps may become impossible.

AN OMINOUS FUTURE

If what you have read so far is causing some angst, you are not alone. A lot of companies feel this sense of doom, even if they can't put their fingers on precisely why and even if they do not realize how ominous it really is. For most of them, the angst is not so much about an impending death or decomposition but about having lost a sense of control.

"Don't look now," write George Colony and Peter Burris of Forrester Research, "but your company is losing control. That message may not have reached your technology management leaders and teams yet, but your marketing brethren already live the challenge. Customers are now in the driver's seat."[13] Forrester is one of the world's leading technology and market research companies.

They go on to describe what they see as the three factors that "have conspired to put your customers on top: (1) ubiquitous information about products, services, and prices; (2) technologies that make them visible and powerful critics; and (3) the ability to purchase from anyone at any time." Indeed, it is all that . . . and more, as you will read here.

Colony and Burris also quote Rick Wagoner, the former CEO of General Motors, speaking at a Forrester Forum: "We used to 'own' the customer. Now we hope and pray that they want to 'own' us."

What a dramatic reversal of control. The real threat is that if you have lost control and fail to get it back quickly, your business *will* die—even if it dies through decomposition.

What does it look like for a business to decompose? It is what happens when you cannot bring new offerings to market in a way that keeps your customers engaged. It is the outcome of your customer satisfaction scores trending in a downward spiral. It is your fate when you can only find people who have heard how difficult it is to do business with you. Or maybe your expense ratios are out of control, and when you try to fix them, your customers rebel—because you have taken steps that mess with them directly. Maybe you try to improve efficiency on the backs of your customers by seeking to influence their behavior in ways they just do not and will not accept. You impose limitations they object to. Perhaps you load on more fees, which they object to—remember the fiasco of banks charging customers to talk to a teller?! What a way to drive efficiency by punishing your customers instead of encouraging them to do the things that will be more efficient but that they will also enjoy!

Cellphone providers right and left have been cutting out unlimited data plans. This was an important element of the relationship customers have with their cellphone companies, and in making this change providers are putting a gun to the head of their customers. Do cellphone companies really think that people who once had unlimited plans aren't going to react negatively to having their data access metered? Or become open to switching to operators who are prepared to use this as a competitive advantage and play on the extra frustration that comes from having customers see some freedom they desire become limited. By the time you read this, they will have already learned just how wrong a calculation they made.

U.S. cellphone providers failed to anticipate this problem when they first began to roll out their plans for smartphones. They did not predict how the use of data would evolve on those smartphones. The European companies hedged, rarely offering a totally unlimited data usage plan. So, the U.S. firms will be blamed for taking something away from customers, and the Europeans will not. Some say the mistake was about expense ratios, but more likely it was sloppiness in product introduction—an ungrounded anticipation of the market and the subsequent cost or retrenching. But whatever the reason, it is not a situation you ever want to put yourself in.

Have you ever met anyone who actually likes paying taxes? Yet, companies continually impose taxes on their customers. Exorbitant overdraft fees at banks. Roaming charges on your cellphone. You travel to Canada, make some calls, and the next thing you know you have an extra $300 on your bill because you did not have the right plan.

ARE YOU PROVOKING YOUR CUSTOMERS?

Whenever businesses reflexively set things up to herd customers into certain group behaviors, they create disdain and dissatisfaction. Customers in general do not react well to these kinds of things. Gen C customers broadcast their disdain into their social worlds. They have a natural inclination against being thought of in a purely transactional way. They don't like it when you treat them like prisoners to *your* conception of how to do business with them.

Of course, if you are losing control of your customers because you are not doing a very good job of meeting their expectations, there are plenty of models you can turn to for clues on what it takes to make customers very loyal. Take the Apple Stores. Go by the Apple Store in Boston and you will see how easy it is for Apple to make customers happy. People are lined up outside the store before it opens, hoping to see someone at the Genius Bar, where Apple provides free-of-charge service advice and training on all of its products. Someone will come out and talk to each person waiting, suggesting that she or he make an appointment rather than wait. The appointment is booked on an iPad for, say, 20 or 30 minutes after the store opens. The employee suggests you wait somewhere more comfortable, like the nearby Starbucks. When you return at the appointed time, you're seen at the Genius Bar. On the spot. Or, if things are really busy, the employee who came outside promises to call at a certain time to let you know of available appointments. And he calls you at that precise time.

How difficult can any of that be? Not too hard, it would seem . . . but it does take a very conscious change of mind-set. Apple, rather than putting the burden on its customer, engages its customers *pro-actively* while always looking at how it engages from the customer's perspective.

Still, it is not as simple as emulating Apple. Just as you are taking steps to ensure your survival from the Gen C onslaught, the whole thing is about to spin away again. It turns out there is a newer and even more ferocious threat at your doorstep, because if Gen C represents a daunting challenge to retain customers who, once lost, you may never get back, what follows in the evolutionary development of customers ought to terrify you.

WELCOME TO THE NIGHTMARE

Gen C customers may just hate you. The up-and-coming generation of customers may choose the path of trying to kill you.

These new customers are blowing up the very notion of Customer Relationship Management. They are not interested in a relationship. They most certainly do not accept being managed. And if that doesn't sound ominous enough, they don't even waste a minute hating doing business with you, like Gen C customers would. They can't hate being your customer, because they reject the very notion of being a customer of anyone—period. A customer, they believe, is someone businesses try to control. These up-and-comers expect to be the ones in control.

No, I am not describing Generation Z, one of the names given to people born from the early 2000s to the present day to distinguish them from Millennials or Generation Y. You may have heard some of the other names that have been given to this group, because the name that will emerge as the leader seems still to be up for grabs.[14] Other names have included the Homeland Generation, Generation@, Net Generation, and iGeneration. A noted marketing firm has proposed the Pluralist Generation, or Plurals. In my view, all these names are wrong. These people, when they talk of Generation Z (by whatever name) are really talking about Gen C-2. And in doing so, they are *missing a lot!*

Just as Gen C includes a characterization within its very name, so, too, does this next generation. Meet Generation D. The members of Gen D are the true envoys of the customerpocalypse. The behaviors of Gen C-2 are the early, emerging behaviors to which many of Gen D's characteristics can be traced. As you learn more about them, and realize how unprepared you are for their ascendancy, you may rightly think of that D as "doom" or "death" or "destruction." To understand how they work, think of the D as standing for three things, depending on the moment: *discover, devour, demonize.*

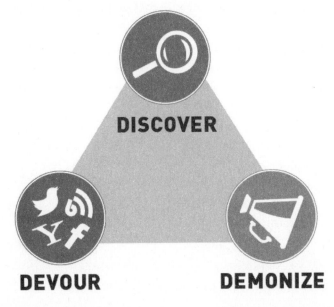

DISCOVER

DEVOUR   **DEMONIZE**

Fail a Gen D customer and you will be lucky to get something like the Facebook post from earlier in this chapter about the restaurant. More likely, the post will be something like this sent out on Twitter:

> never doing business again with _____ bank totally f **ked my account went to _____ bank and switched accounts great experience recommended—you should do the same!

The tweet is then retweeted and seen by thousands. Before you can do anything about it, you have been demonized.

Microsoft got a Gen D taste of what Netflix suffered in the earlier example. In June 2013, the company released the latest version of its popular game console Xbox, known as Xbox One. Customers who purchased it would be required to have an Internet connection to play offline games. On top of that, Microsoft imposed some restrictions on how used games could be shared. The result: "disappointed Xbox fans immediately expressed outrage across social media following the news."[15] It took only a few days for the president of Microsoft's Interactive Entertainment Business, Don Mattrick, to announce a reversal. It included a very important point, particularly about the used games.

Addressing Xbox One customers, Mattrick wrote, "The ability to lend, share, and resell these games at your discretion is of incredible importance to you."[16] Gen D had made a big point, and scored a big victory, about _ownership_ and how this young generation views the issue. Would the Xbox One be enjoying its tremendous market success had Microsoft stood by its original plan rather than listen to its customers?

Colony and Burris put things well, describing how today's situation "puts the heat on twenty-first-century institutions, causing disruption and discontinuities. Traditional sources of sustainable returns melt in the glare of increasing customer power. That brand new story you spent $18 million telling? It just got undercut by a single influential blogger compiling a list of 12 counter-examples that has been retweeted 1.2 million times and picked up by the newswires."[17]

As Benjamin Franklin famously noted, "It takes many good deeds to build a reputation and only one bad one to lose it."

"Don't Sell to Me!"

Gen D does not want to be sold to. Being sold to is like being controlled. No, the seamless experience they desire with your business, to which they would probably never admit, is based on wanting to discover you and your product or service. So, on top of all that connectivity, you have to figure out how to facilitate their discovery, proactively but invisibly, to create the illusion that they are discovering all on their own. They are looking for something that makes even connectivity and connective collaboration seem old-fashioned, and they want that invisible magic. They want *radical authenticity*, and when they discover something they like, they devour it.

If you are older than Gen D (and even Gen C), you have most likely always had relatively low expectations for your relationship with the bank, the phone company, or any other business with which you deal. When you learn your bank contributed to the financial meltdown by selling your mortgage as part of a bundle of securities in an effort to make a quick profit, you may despise it and you might even take some political action like voting or even protesting. But while you probably don't see it as a personal betrayal by another human being, a Gen D customer may.

Gen D redefines loyalty. The totems or artifacts of loyalty have changed drastically in the run-up to Gen D's emergence. At banks, those artifacts once were passbooks for savings accounts, which have gone the way of the dinosaurs. At grocery stores, a half a century ago, they were S&H Green Stamps, collected over time with purchases and redeemed—as a gift for your loyalty—for things you would never just go out and buy. Green Stamps were a physical manifestation that led customers to the belief that they did not just make purchases at the grocery store but that they would be rewarded with something in return. The customer and the store were building value together. Today, that artifact has disappeared, replaced by the automatic discount on specific items at the store when you hand over your savings card, which also gives the store the capability to track your every purchase for future and even instant marketing in the form of on-the-spot coupons.

These are examples of transactional loyalty systems. Gen C might accept the word "loyalty" in that context. Gen D members want nothing to do with the idea of loyalty, as such. While most companies are grappling with connectivity and the challenge of Gen C custom-ers, these new Gen D customers want nothing short of trust, trans-parency, and total openness. If they want loyalty, and expressed it as such, they would say it is *your* loyalty to *them*. The authenticity they demand is visceral, and if they sense that you are trying to make them *think* you are giving them autonomy but are really trying to sneak some M (for management) into the equation, they will have a prob-lem, and you will have a bigger problem.

Another characteristic of this generation is that their reactions vac-illate between extremes. Their discovery and experience of you may cause them rapture, which means they want to devour you (in a good way), but it can just as easily cause them to demonize you. We saw the beginnings of this demonization more generally in Gen C, but the Gen C reaction is more on the passive-aggressive side. They post about you, drop you, and the relationship is over. The worst "D" you might get from this is to be summarily *dismissed*.

Gen D, though, takes things to a different level, at both extremes. They experience amazing levels of affection with products and compa-nies, even if they don't see them as products and companies. They're in love. They love Apple, for instance, in a kind of embodiment of the "I'm a Mac and you're a PC" advertisements of a few years back. You are either great and loved raptly or really untrustworthy, uncool, and, hence, demonized.

This active demonization is a unique characteristic of Gen D and one of the signs of the customerpocalypse. They don't create "suck sites" like those mentioned earlier, because those are meant to push people in a certain direction. Gen D is a generation of people who *pull*. While members of Gen C shoot their experiences out into the world and wait for you to come to them for details, Gen D puts it in your face and drags you down.

We asked a group of Gen D members ages 14 to 22 whether they have either promoted or complained about a product themselves.

One young woman said, "I must do that about 700 million times a day. You talk about things you like. I just went to a sale at Gap last weekend. 'Look, I got this cute skirt. They have a lot of cute stuff there right now'—or something. My friends will tell me that they went to this restaurant, and they had a really good drink special."

The power and importance of these kinds of connections is backed up by the research. The Nielsen Global Trust in Advertising Survey, conducted in late 2011, involved 28,000 Internet respondents in 56 countries and found that 92 percent of consumers "around the world say they trust earned media . . . above all other forms of advertising— an increase of 18 percent since 2007 . . ." Earned media is "word-of-mouth and recommendations from friends and family."[18]

"It's like your friends are the ones advertising the thing for you," added a young man. "If a friend posted on Facebook that he uses a product, I'd be more likely to believe it and want to use it versus seeing a commercial—because it's someone's word versus a company that's paying money for [the ad]."

As Michael Maoz, a Gartner analyst and noted thought leader on customer service, states, "Trust remains a cornerstone of an engaged customer. Although customers may remain customers even when they do not trust an organization, it is less costly and customer actions are more predictable when customers trust the enterprise. Other emotional factors that the customer service organization should attempt to achieve are a sense of enjoyment, commitment to solve customer issues, a sense of empathy and understanding, and leaving customers with a feeling of contentment that their problems were dealt with swiftly and with the least effort."[19]

Again, *authenticity*. "That's definitely more effective," chimed in some of the young women.[20]

One thing Gen D does do that is really quite different is to celebrate the fail, actively. They are the generation most associated with the meme of the "epic fail" on social media sites. They see it as a gotcha moment to share with their friends (and friends is broadly defined to include everyone they've ever known, or who is known by someone they know, or who they have no relationship with other than what appears to the rest of us to be the narrowest sliver of obscure commonality). These are young people who don't mind experiencing failure because they get to post or tweet about it. Gen C creates a United Sucks page on Facebook[21] and stops at that. An example of an early Gen D-like behavior is recording "United Breaks Guitars," posting it on YouTube, watching as it goes viral (with nearly 13 million hits as of this writing[22]), and then even publishing a book about the experience.[23] Gen D launches an all-out war without any regard for the consequences to the opponent but with a distinct—if not explicitly stated—personal interest based on the heightened sense of entitlement that characterizes this group.

GENERATION C

Wikipedia

Facebook
(unmediated; everyone is a "friend")

Online dating

Fan chat rooms

Laments online bullying

Gives away privacy for consumer benefits, often unknowingly

Tweets or Facebooks occasional customer service complaints

Brand loyal

Watches cable channels

GENERATION D

Wikileaks

Reddit
(mediated; rigorous peer ranking)

Online community organizing

Fan fiction

Reposts and retweets a list of online bullies

Understand privacy implications and manipulate for their own benefits

Builds elaborate "fake-brand" or videos to voice their disatisfaction

Doesn't see a brand; see themselves in brands they embrace

Streams media over the Internet

This up-and-coming generation makes the digital connectedness of its predecessors seem mild by comparison. For example, the group of Gen D members I mentioned earlier happened to meet just a few days after the death of Nelson Mandela. They were asked how they had learned about his passing. Most said Tumblr or Instagram.

As one teenage girl said, "Eighty percent of the time, if I tell you something, I read it on Instagram."[24]

Another young woman explained the process by which online information gets disseminated among her peers. "If something happens, I'll kinda see a vague post maybe first, and I'll be like 'that's weird,' and then I'll see something else related to it, and I'll be like 'what's going on?' Then I'll keep scrolling and I'll see something else, like the actual news article, or somebody specifically saying what's going on. But like, everybody's just talking about it."

And just to drive home the connectedness issue with Gen D, consider the answers Gen D members gave our facilitator when he asked if anyone had ever lost or broken a mobile phone.

"It was painful," said one young woman.

A teenage boy explained, "You feel alone in the world, and you're useless and can't do anything. I'm so lonely without my phone, and like, what am I gonna do?"

"I freak out," added another of the Gen D members.

"I bring my charger with me," said one of the young men.

"I left it at my house for a day," a young woman chimed in, "and I'm like—I can't even listen to music now. How am I gonna live?"

To Gen D, being connected has become fundamental to their very *existence*, and hence being unconnected is an existential crisis.

"I think the most annoying thing about not having a phone is [this]," said one of the teenage girls. "That's the only time I ever go on social networks and stuff. So, it's really aggravating when I have lots of friends [asking] 'I tweeted you the other day, and why haven't you been answering me? Where have you been? Oh, have you seen anything on Instagram?' No. Nope. I don't have my phone right now. I lost my phone."

Friends' expectations around social media are "pretty high," report the Gen D members we spoke to. There is a lesson in that for anyone who wants to connect with these customers.

ANTHROPOMORPHISM

Those classic "I'm a Mac and you're a PC" commercials speak to a particular way in which the rapture and devouring manifests itself with Gen D customers. When they truly love a brand, they no longer see a brand. Their identity with the brand goes way beyond brand *loyalty*; they become the brand, and the brand becomes them.

Lush, a cosmetics company based in England, is a good example of this sort of rapture and devour behavior. The company began in 1994 with one store and today has more than 800 in more than 50 countries. Lush sells a variety of handmade products it produces on its own, from soaps to shampoos to shower gels, lotions, and more. Everything is made naturally. Lush products are completely vegetarian, nearly completely vegan, and some 60 percent free of preservatives. Not only has the company made a big deal about not using any animal fats in its products, but Lush has also become a force in the anti-animal-testing community. All Lush products are tested exclusively on human volunteers, and the company refuses to buy anything from any company even remotely involved with animal testing. Pushing corporate responsibility to a limit beyond even some of the most forward-thinking companies, Lush offers a free face mask to anyone who returns five or more used Lush containers to the store and has a public goal to have 100 percent of all the company's packaging "easily recyclable, compostable, or biodegradable."

The company also gives a lot of money to a wide variety of causes that are not strictly environmental (at least in the traditional sense). You can be sure Gen D members are well aware of this, which is part of why they love Lush. To them, Lush is not a company. It's not even a brand *per se*. It is a part of their lives.

Using the word "awesome" to describe Lush, one of the young Gen D women we spoke to said, "It's a lifestyle, actually."[25]

Even with all its ethical roots, there seems to be nothing particularly preachy about how Lush works.

If you have ever gone into a Lush store, you have seen some of what makes the brand rapturous to young women in Gen D. The sales clerks are Gen D. They are not pushy. They are energetic, and it's difficult to imagine they are actually working. It looks as if they are just hanging out, having fun and showing friends a bunch of stuff they love. Then there is the manner in which things are displayed. One marketing expert has compared it to the way fruit sellers display their wares. Everything's out and unwrapped. You can pick it up and choose the size and shape of a particular piece of soap, which adds to the sense of discovery. Lush has even called itself a "cosmetics grocer."

"I think what helps is that the stores are fabulously fragrant and smell so beautiful when you walk right in," said one teenage girl.

"All the packaging is wonderful," added another. "The products themselves are so good . . . I bought a bath bomb maybe like two weeks ago, and I used it, and I was just like—I'm a princess now. This is wonderful, and I want to tell everybody about this experience so they can have it too."

Lush is truly close to its customers. As Mark Wolverton, president of Lush North America, explains, "We don't want a store where customers come in and browse and then take their products to the salesperson behind the till. Our staff ask questions about skin and hair type and make a big fuss over each customer, so it's fun and they have a great experience."[26] For Gen D girls, it's like having a sleepover.

Also, Lush gets how important it is to have authentic connections with customers. One of the young women among the Gen D members we spoke to described why she follows Lush's Twitter feed. "I tweeted at them about something, that I really liked their product . . . I'd been using it a lot. It was something I was really happy with, and I wanted my friends and people that I have on Twitter to know I'm using this thing and I like it, and where to get it. And [Lush] tweeted me back, which was exciting because nobody ever does that."[27]

Loyalty deepens when you acknowledge the social vote given to you by Gen D.

If Lush is rapture, something Gen D wants to devour, what then is an example of the demon? Well, just imagine how a Gen D member feels when he looks at something online as a potential purchase, and then little advertisements for that item or similar items keep popping up wherever he goes on the Web, over and over. Perhaps that has happened to you. You search for a new blender, for instance, and the next thing you know you are being followed around for days and days on the Web by an annoying little blender advertisement. What could be more opposite of "invisible" or "magic"? Even if you are not a member of Gen D, you probably resent this. When we first saw Tom Cruise in the futuristic film *Minority Report* in 2002 being greeted with personal offers as he walked down a glass corridor, it was cool; now it seems problematic, dated, and intrusive.

When we got Gen D members together, one of the things we discussed was online advertising.[28] Asked about how they respond to the ads that show up on YouTube just before they can watch a selected video, one teenager was clear. "I hate it." Turning to the rest of the group, he asked, "Right?"

Most said they skip the ads. One young woman was more specific. "Wait the five seconds, then skip the ad immediately."

"Sometime I can't even wait the five seconds," a young man responded.

The most detailed response to the question revealed just how much of a chance you have with Gen D. One teenage girl explained that despite her lack of specific knowledge about how marketing is supposed to work traditionally, "it's like they have those five seconds that you have to watch before you can choose to skip. So I was actually thinking about it one day and I'm like, companies need to make those five seconds really count. So sometimes I'll continue to watch [if] in those five seconds you made it really, really extravagant and wonderful. Let me see what this is about."

She continued. "I know I'm weird for doing that. But sometimes I do sit there, and I'll watch the whole thing because that first five seconds was so good. But most of the time, yeah, I just skip it."[29]

The message here: *you've got a maximum of five seconds to capture the attention of Gen D!*

YouTube, though, sometimes will not let you skip the ads. You are forced to watch the entire ad. So, what do these Gen D members do? Most we spoke to rejected the idea of skipping; they had picked a video to watch and they wanted to see it. They'll mute an ad if it goes on for 20 or 30 seconds, but longer?

"I reload," said another young woman," and sometimes it'll go away."

A teenage boy explained, "See if you get a better ad."

"But it's kinda sad," said a teenage girl, "because that's people's job. It's sad that what commercials and ads have turned into—it's just like, ugh. God! I want to skip it."

Another young woman agreed. "Commercials," she declared, "are the least effective form of marketing for me by far." There was a chorus of agreement, and hatred for commercials—"on TV, at the movies . . . on the radio, on YouTube—it doesn't matter."

The companies that are advertising to these Gen D members are making them angry by wasting their time and violating their need to be in control of discovery. "I'm in the middle of doing something that I want to do," said one of the teenagers. "I want to listen to the radio. I want to watch this movie. So you're gonna interrupt what I purposely came here to do to tell me about your—no! I'm not gonna care about it now."

You—the advertiser—have been demonized. You have been subjected to one meaning of Gen D's "D."

There are ways around this, like how Lush operates. While demon brands are busy trying to sell to the customer, Lush lets customers discover on their own. This is how Gen D wants it to work: they discover new brands and take pride when they discover something *unadvertised*, be it something known only through social media, something funded through Kickstarter, some entertainment distributed through crowd sourcing, or a consumer variant on flash mobs and meet-ups.

Let's look more closely at this new pattern of discovery.

"I WANT TO BE THE DISCOVERER!"

Gen D is very quick to form impressions, often influenced by elements borrowed from others, and they are quick to make decisions. They are willing to act on their discoveries. The members of Gen D are immersed in streams of information. They are bombarded by activity feeds and tweets and other sorts of things that have already been customized to target them directly. Given that reality, you would think they recognize that they are not discovering on their own. But they want to believe that they and their friends *are* the discoverers. This turns even the most advanced notions of proactive marketing on their heads and raises all sorts of issues for search engine optimization. You have to lay out honey pots in new and interesting ways so that these consumers will come upon them and never sense they were led to them. No pushing and no overt seduction. No chasing them around the Internet like that blender.

Thinking more about this, an old-school fishing analogy comes to mind. Traditional marketing is like drag fishing the bottom, with broad nets that not only pull up every possible fish but also grab license plates or whatever else may be lurking on the ocean floor. You drag around and just see what comes up. The best of the more proactive marketing is like spear fishing. You get to evaluate the surroundings, pick a target, pursue, and catch. But dealing with Gen D is more like fly fishing. Those who fly fish will tell you that the fish selects the fly not the other way around—and it's the fish's decision and action that gets it hooked. You have to be willing to spend a lot of time being patient as you tie flies, and then being more patient as you stand in the river with the fish, thinking all day about what might appeal to a fish. You spend hours thinking about a fish—all without disturbing the pristine setting. You may catch nothing and go home with an empty creel. Nonetheless, the shared perception must not be that you are a still, silent, hungry hunter, but instead you are a coparticipant in a shared experience. As the fish see you leaving, they "hear" you proclaim that it was a great day, even if you caught nothing.

Gen D members are like those fish. They need to hear you proclaim that engaging with them in any way, shape, or form was great . . . even if it's not how you really feel. In addition, just like with the fish (where you are not supposed to be selling), your approach with Gen D has to be "catch and release." In other words, you need to earn your next strike—from scratch—with another brilliant lure.

Now *that's* discovery!

The Gen D "devour-or-demonize" characteristic changes everything about how you anticipate consumers might be led to anthropomorphize your business. Gen D ascribes human attributes and feelings to the businesses they choose to engage with, even if they never deal with the same person twice. The businesses that have figured this out are the ones that make sure every time a customer deals with them, each and every one of their employees is part of an engaged, and engaging, organism. It's the Lush retail store. It's the Genius Bar at the Apple Store.

These companies embrace being anthropomorphized as well, ensuring that the brand has a consistent personality across channels and experiences, which enables people to associate the brand with a value system they like and support. Contrast that with the businesses that come across as schizophrenic and end up being customerpocalpytically disdained and demonized.

Gen D also creates an imperative to rethink the meaning of privacy, because there is strong evidence they have a very different conception of privacy than most of us are used to. Privacy has a different value to them; in fact, Gen D consumers are remarkably open to giving up what most of us as see as privacy. This trend began with their Gen C precursors. Just consider the sorts of things they post on Facebook.

Gen D will let you watch them browse. In return, they expect that you won't try selling to them. They also expect you not to waste their time, and they might define wasted time in much smaller increments than you are used to. A teenager among the Gen D members we spoke to bemoaned how one online service he uses wastes his time with an ineffective recommendation engine (although he didn't use that term).

"Netflix thinks that I really like '70s and '80s horror films *and My Little Pony*," he said, mockingly. "I'm sure there's a demographic for that somewhere."[30]

Even ridiculous recommendations are obviously based on some kind of data, the topic of Chapter 2.

Generation D members are also highly sensitive to anything that appears to be you *taking* their privacy. The Gen D privacy line seems to be situated right at the point where they think you might be profiting from their information. (Of course, they are smart enough to know that you probably are, so you really want to steer clear of anything that makes them stop and think about it.)

All of these changes have contributed to why your business may already be decomposing. Being seen as uncool could be the trigger. A failure to retool your business to meet the expectations of Gen C may be the trigger. As if that weren't bad enough, add the halo effect Gen D has on Gen C and even people of older generations. With the stage set by Gen C for the ascendant Gen D, we are all being drawn into their online social world, with all of what that means for us as consumers.

Yes, Gen C and Gen D are driving companies to the brink. Some companies don't even realize it. They fail to see how important it is to change how they "intrude" on people. They don't understand just how intrusive customers, existing and potential, consider those injected online advertisements. No matter the upside in terms of driving business their way, these companies may be gambling with a very significant downside that could spell the beginning of their end.

Is yours one of those companies? Demographic reality is barreling down on you like a runaway train, driven by new digital technologies in what Forrester Research has aptly dubbed "the age of the customer"—defined as "a 20-year business cycle in which the most successful enterprises will reinvent themselves to systematically understand and serve increasingly powerful customers."[31]

Gen D is your future. The coming customerpocalypse means your time is limited unless you make a dramatic change in the way you think about customers and customer engagement. This kind of change is absolutely fundamental to the continuity of your business, both because your customers demand it and your competitors are sharpening their knives. Incremental change will not do the trick, unless it is increments of a larger radical transformation over time—and a relatively short time, at that. Incremental change absent this overall intellectual transformation will not work, because the nature of the change simply does not lend itself to incremental thinking. The dramatic change required means you have to assume a very different intellectual vantage point, and any incremental change must be in the context of transformation or you will hit the wrong target.

Let's take a look at how businesses got to this point, where they actually face destruction from the very customers and customerpocalypse they should be preparing for, beginning with the biggest elephant in the room—data.

2

DEATH BY DATA

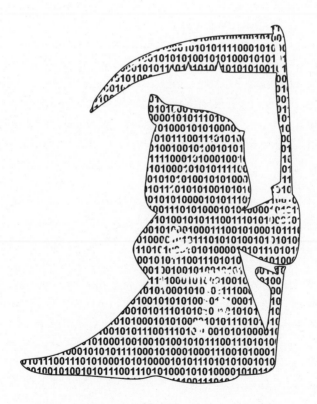

Data can kill your business. Cost data is particularly deadly. It's the easiest to gather and the most dangerous to apply. It becomes very easy to see what a customer is doing that costs your business money, and to calibrate how different practices might be less expensive. Responding to this without proper context can impose ultimately self-destructive changes on how you engage with customers, because that response is based on an incomplete understanding of the consequences. Consider an early cautionary tale that is periodically recycled through analogous missteps by tone-deaf companies.

In the mid-1990s, First National Bank of Chicago looked at some of the information it had been gathering about its customers and decided to try influencing their behavior in a way that would cut costs. The bank wanted to drive customers to its automated "Bank-by-Phone" system, which was a money saver for First Chicago, so it imposed a $2 charge on customers who wanted to get account information from a live Customer Service Representative.[1]

It's not surprising that First Chicago is long gone. Imagine telling a Gen C customer she has to pay to speak to someone in your enterprise. Then imagine trying to do business that way with a Gen D customer! But First Chicago embraced and assertively advocated this idea of influencing customer behavior, arguing that the bank's new policy was, in fact, good customer service because it would encourage the very behavior it believed most beneficial to the bank.

Instead, what First Chicago did was *disenfranchise* its customers.

Eventually, the charges disappeared. But the idea of charging customers fees to influence their behavior did not go away. Some business sectors became especially aggressive, trying to charge customers a fee for everything they could think of. Think airlines: Fees for checked baggage, when first introduced, were both aimed at increasing revenue and considered a way to discourage passengers from bringing stuff on trips that make the airplanes heavier and thus increase fuel costs at a time when those costs were skyrocketing.

Again, the aim was to change customer behavior. The culmination may well be Ireland-based no-frills Ryanair's announcement in 2010 that it would charge to use the bathroom on its flights. "Stephen McNamara, spokesperson for the airline, told TravelMail: 'By charging for the toilets we are hoping to change passenger behaviour so that they use the bathroom before or after the flight.'"[2]

Fortunately, the Ryanair plan was aborted, just like the First Chicago fee to talk to a real live person. But what hasn't disappeared are the mechanized and unresponsive Voice Response Units each of us have to contend with every day when we try to do business. These are more of the same, imposing a behavior change when you just want to talk to someone living and breathing. No wonder nearly everyone has a visceral hatred for these systems.

There are so many other stories of bad, bad decisions being made because of cost data. Since the advent of Frederick Winslow Taylor's "scientific management" (also known as Taylorism) back in the nineteenth century, businesses have sought to improve their economic efficiency by breaking down everything about the business into the smallest parts that could be analyzed and gathering information about how much those parts cost. Companies gather cost data about goods, processes, waste, customers . . . you name it. The prevalence of cost data is buttressed by accounting systems that make it easily available to decision makers. But as the tales above show, it's a most unfortunate place to start when dealing with customers.

The data you choose to focus on can drive you to make some really bad decisions about your customers and about influencing their behavior. Gen D customers don't just reject being told how to behave; they will tell the world you are trying to manipulate them.

In both the Netflix and Xbox One missteps described in Chapter 1, data played a destructive role. In Microsoft's case, "the data suggested it made business sense to require Xbox One to have Internet to protect Microsoft from piracy. In the case of Netflix, the data also showed that streaming video is the future, so separating the streaming service into a separate company made sense as well."[3]

Even with lessons like these, the core of how most companies structure their relationships with their customers continues to be based on customer *data*. Lots of data. Tons of data. Megadata. Metadata. Businesspeople love data. They are addicted to it. It's tangible. It's reassuring.

As you accumulate more and more data, though, you need to ask yourself whether the way around the bad decisions that too often result from a data focus is to use even *more* data. If decisions based on increasing access to data are turning out badly, what is going to happen when you add more data to the mix?

Big Data, Bigger Problem

Big Data is a loosely used term in information technology used to describe sets of data that are so dauntingly large, so harrowingly complex, that mere mortals can only work with them through highly sophisticated systems. While storing big data is no longer the challenge it once was, the challenge of searching through it, analyzing it, sharing it, and—quite frankly—making heads or tails of it has only been exacerbated as the amount of data has grown exponentially. But in a typical case of the tail wagging the dog, the capacity and capability of information technology on the purely technological side keeps making the problem of big data bigger and bigger. We are on our way from the terabyte to the yottabyte, which equals 1 septillion bytes (a septillion, by the way, has 24 zeros).

Just in case you doubt the inexorable march to bigger and bigger data storage, consider the news in late January 2013 from a group of researchers at the European Bioinformatics Institute. They reported that they had succeeded in storing digital information in synthetic DNA molecules and then were able to recreate the original data files without error. Sure, it was only 739 kilobytes, but "the researchers said their new technique, which includes error-correction software, was a step toward a digital archival storage medium of immense scale. Their goal is a system that will safely store the equivalent of one million CDs in a gram of DNA for 10,000 years."[4]

For businesses, big data is not a cost issue. The plummeting cost of data storage ensures that, but—as technology facilitates the aggregation of more and more data—is anyone really thinking about what data represents? Are you thinking about more and more data and what good it might do you in a world of Gen D customers?

AUTOPSY OF THE "CUSTOMER SERVICE MOVEMENT"

Businesspeople have been gathering data about customers for a long time. You can see why they can fall so easily into the trap that "more of the same" will halt the impending customerpocalypse. After all, data has been at the center of just about every aspect of how companies have tried to figure out how best to deal with their customers over the decades. They've gone from ad-hoc approaches to more disciplined approaches to full-blown programs centered on customer "engagement" and customer "relationships." Eventually, an entire industry emerged around what is called Customer Relationship Management (CRM). Note that nasty word "management" that Gen D abhors, which was supposed to create alignment with customers *wherever* they were heading and thus prevent the very demonization and destruction described in Chapter 1.

CRM is the source for a very important *false* promise about data. It concerns the infamous 360-degree view of the customer. The concept of 360 comes from the number of degrees in a circle and implies that if you can put your customer in the middle of a circle, you can gather up all the data about that customer to see him or her from every possible angle, creating the basis for deep understanding of customer needs. Here is a rather typical definition of 360-degree view of the customer that comes from an online dictionary.

A 360-degree customer view offers a total view of the customer relationship dynamic for a business.[5]

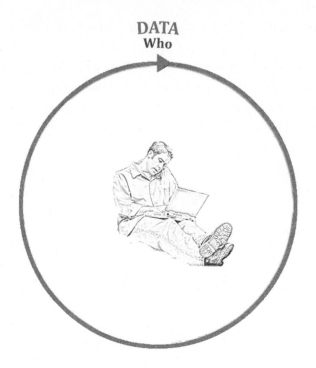

DATA
Who

Now, facilitating customer engagement with that customer's data can be helpful, but no customer is a standalone amoeba swimming in a round petri dish. Putting a customer in the 360 view typically shows you nothing about how that customer is part of a larger "organism," a network of networks that are familial, business, and social. You can peer at the customer in the middle of the petri dish all day and all night, but you are not necessarily going to see any of that network. In other words, the 360 view alone may be interesting, but it is indubitably incomplete.

Still, the concept of the 360-degree customer view permeates the business world. It's everywhere. A recent Google search on "360 customer" got 428 million hits. But it has a rather checkered history, having developed out of a customer service movement that spawned all manner of approaches to handling customers—as in the First Chicago example, not all of them very customer-oriented.

Another trend that emerged in the customer service movement and CRM, which is linked to cost data and treating customer service as a cost center, was the industrialization of customer service and its eventual outsourcing. Overseas call centers debuted with poorly trained, transient staff with cultural and language differences that drove customers crazy—and still do. Even customer service organizations that corrected the worst and most persistent problems typically found that staffing their call centers with the "right" people didn't help. These people still lacked the tools needed to do their jobs well.

It is important to note that the problem is not just that information about costs can lead to simplistic, bad decisions about customers. The problem runs deeper. It's not what data is *about*, but what data actually *is*.

DATA IS ONLY MEMORY

Here is the first thing you need to know about data. It is about the past. Data is memory and *only* memory. The storage facilities for data are like our human brains, packed full of memory. Now, forget about your business for a moment. Think about your life. To what extent are the things that make you an effective individual based exclusively on your memory? And doesn't memory's retrospective nature foster decision patterns that may not be applicable in the present or future? What about making decisions about how to deal with new people you meet? Could all this data be a seductive comfort that misses much of what is fully required?

Those questions are missed in businesses that overrely on data. And still, companies that are in danger of exploding continue to listen to the hardware hawkers who tell them they need to get these massive storage machines and fill them with every possible piece of data they can accumulate!

Again, ask yourself: Is more necessarily better? One thing for sure is that more data does not automatically translate into a better view of the customer. To be effective, 360 is supposed to accommodate all the information about a customer across time and across locale. It needs to incorporate all sorts of data, such as the history of transactions, the history of marketing interactions, the history of every sales call and service call, the history of every complaint or compliment, the results of every survey, and so on. Notice again that "history" and "results" are about the past.

Even for one customer, the sheer mass of data can become very, very difficult for people to navigate, understand, and interpret quickly enough for it to do any good. How do you understand the data? Can you do a time-series analysis quickly? Does your Customer Service Representative know how to use it all? Does she even have time to wade through it while talking to a customer?

Data rapidly becomes overwhelming, particularly when you want to deal with the whole customer. And it needs to be used all over the place, in many different venues throughout your business. There is the front office, back office, contact center, perhaps the point of contact with the customer in a bricks-and-mortar store, and so on.

Plus, data is really nothing without context. In reality, it only tells you *who* the customer is. Context includes, for instance, all the links that are relevant to a given customer. If your daughter calls to get a quote from your insurance company, with which you have done business for decades, she ought to be treated as part of your valued family network. If the insurer has every conceivable piece of data about you, but does not recognize that she's your daughter (her last name might be different, which is only the beginning of the challenge), the possibility that your customer service rep will mess things up increases. That list of histories did not include information about family members or other business relationships that might be relevant. The traditional advocates of CRM and of accumulating more and more data have focused on quantity at the expense of distilling what people see into the right context for each venue.

These kinds of problems have existed since the beginning of CRM, and the advocates of Big Data are not proposing anything to make them go away. You still have to figure out how to accumulate so much data. You still have to go get it from lots of different places, which is a daunting task. It's still very difficult to train people to do the right things with whatever data you give them to work with. It's a big enough challenge just to train people to look at data and form an opinion. It's nearly impossible to train those same people to look at more and more data and understand coherently what has changed over time. And change it will, a lot, if you collect every available piece of data about every existing or potential customer.

To be fair, the traditional CRM and 360 advocates try to keep up with new and "better" technologies. There are hybrid combinations of data warehousing and real-time information gathering. All the attention to the technical aspects of working with more and more data comes, it seems, at the expense of the needed focus on how to apply the information we already have.

DATA SUICIDE

Let's be clear: Huge amounts of data do not translate into an automatic death sentence. You don't drown in all circumstances. It's like swimming in the ocean. There is a lot of water, but the mere fact that you dive in, or sail across it, does not automatically mean your death. You can swim. You can navigate. You might even get away with drinking a bit of it to slake your thirst, but since it is salt water, that's not going to last very long.

Data is far more diverse than the water of the ocean. And that is why even some accomplished data "swimmers" and "navigators" among big companies are dying or have already died while swimming in data. Sometimes, the way businesses use their customer data is the equivalent of committing suicide.

Some of the best examples are in the realm of information overload for service representatives. After all, people can only internalize and remember so much. These reps become so overwhelmed at the point of contact with customers that they end up not being able to serve customers in the manner those customers wish to be served. A structural failure like that is the beginning of the end for just about any business.

The banking industry provides a really good tale of suicide by data overload. Years ago, banks were desperate to become financial supermarkets. The basic concept was to get the average customer to engage with the bank around a massive collection of financial products, everything from savings accounts to consumer loans to investments and retirement accounts. Put retail banking, business banking, wealth management, brokerage, and, in Citi's case, even trying to put Traveler's Insurance all under one roof. Banking deregulation in the 1990s created good business opportunities, but that does not mean they were pursued well.

People behind financial supermarkets believed they could establish an operations side to the business that could handle every one of the diverse products for these different kinds of banking—from contact centers for credit cards to mortgages. They also believed that customers would want, indeed, that they would crave, these multiline experiences with one big institution. To them, it made perfect sense. They were sure customers would respond favorably and flock to the supermarket.

Why, then, did the experiment fail? On the one hand, customer service staff had access to enormous amounts of aggregated data about customers. They could see every transaction and every product offering. What they had was like a 360-degree view of the customer. More accurately, they had dozens of 360-degree views. Unfortunately, the technological systems they used . . . well, the word is *sucked*. There was no structure to all that data, and the multiple systems that needed to be navigated offered little or no guidance to the staff people who had access to the data. They could not do their jobs effectively, and as they drowned in data, they took the entire notion of the supermarket down into the depths with them.

In truth, the financial supermarket idea itself was not wrong. What was wrong was the blind love of data. They took a data-centric approach to the data and the products, forcing staff to do something at which they simply could not succeed—digest all of the customer data and gauge product suitability to that customer in real time, without adequate help from the technology. So, instead of achieving 360 degrees of clarity, they achieved a blur.

Another type of data suicide occurs when senior management misses the big trends because they are so focused on their own narrow data. That is what happened to Sony, which ignored where its customers were heading. The company looked at its own history and the data that was all about the past, not at where things were going and how consumers were shifting away from physical CDs to digital music files. The company ignored how customers' buying patterns were changing and what that could have told Sony about what it should offer and how to deliver it.

Ironically, Sony could have *owned* the digital music business, from recording through distribution. The company had an inside track, with divisions that covered everything from the record company through the devices. It's a point Steve Jobs makes in his authorized biography; Apple came in and completely disrupted Sony's business.[6] Meanwhile, Sony's corporate leaders maintained an inside-out perspective, obsessed with the company's corporate structure and with protecting company assets while giving hardly a nod to an outside-in (that is, from the customer to the company) point of view.

Once the world leader in personal music entertainment, Sony's Walkman and Discman were outdone not only by technological changes but by how Gen C and its precursors saw their personal relationship with recorded music. Apple figured it out brilliantly, combining data about the past with what it understood about customers' future goals and objectives. In doing so, the iPod and iTunes changed the way business is done, giving new meaning to connectivity in the process. A device, music, a store, access whenever, recommendations that get smarter the more the system is used . . . all seamlessly integrated. So far, this is working for Gen D, but no doubt someone much younger than you and me is figuring out the next disruptive innovation that will put Apple to the test. Perhaps *disruptive* should be added to the many meanings of the D in Gen D. Indeed, recent challengers such as Spotify, Pandora, and Beats Music are gaining share by combining data about an individual's music preferences with information about what others with similar tastes are enjoying—moving data from the category of individual memory to a more reliable collective memory.

The history of business is littered with data suicides. The addiction to data underlies many stories of failure. The obsession with data feeds the false notion that a company is doing well (based on its past), while the impending changes and death threats go unnoticed or ignored. In the broadly defined entertainment industry, for example, companies miss their marks again and again, failing to see where their customers are going and ending up following the dinosaurs into oblivion.

Interestingly, the many examples of death by data seem to have little effect on how businesses operate on the whole. Rather than look beyond data, they employ increasingly complex systems that use customer data in more dynamic ways than ever before, which might have helped Sony. Still, the focus is on data. Businesses are tripping over themselves to capture every bit of customer information they can. They capture the stream of screens you went through on a Website, and every item you looked at but did not purchase, and all the selections you made to the voice-response system on the telephone, and how many seconds you spent on this or that Web page before moving on, and . . . *ad infinitum*. And they do all this because they are absolutely convinced that the data they capture will inform their interactions with their customer in a positive, profitable way.

Creepy Data Gathering

Casting such a wide and indiscriminate net for data can lead you to mess up in new ways you might never have considered before, and in doing so remind Gen C customers why they hate doing business with you and Gen D customers why they don't care whether you live or die. While Gen D customers are willing to share the most intimate details of their lives with their friends through social media, they become highly resentful if they think your business is gathering information about them, especially if you are going to use that to try to sell to them. They will demonize you in a heartbeat.

Facebook got a taste of this in the previous decade. In November 2007, the social Website launched Beacon, which was a part of Facebook's advertisement system. It worked by gathering data about Facebook users from third-party sites such as Yelp, Blockbuster, HotWire, and others of the 44 partner Websites. Some of a Facebook user's activity on the partner sites would then show up in that user's Facebook News Feed.

Not long after its launch, there was a dramatic backlash from users and privacy advocates. And when a report came out that Beacon was collecting data from its partner Websites even about users of those sites who weren't members of Facebook, and there was evidence that activity on the other Websites was being published on Facebook even when a user declined that option specifically, concerns mounted. The controversy led to a class-action lawsuit, and ultimately Facebook shut down Beacon in September 2009.

Two years later, Facebook CEO Mark Zuckerberg characterized Beacon as one of "a small number of high-profile mistakes" that "have often overshadowed much of the good work we've done."[7] Since then, Facebook seems to have learned how to bring advertising into its business model in far less creepy ways.

For companies today, the paradox is this: How do you gather the data the Gen D customer expects you to have, but wants to ignore that you are gathering it or pretend you aren't gathering it at all? And how do you do it in a way that isn't . . . well . . . *creepy*?

Google and other Web-based e-mail services read your mail and mine it for keywords as a way to determine what products you might be interested in purchasing. They are not the only businesses doing this. Your questions on automated voice-response systems are recorded and mined. So, too, are the record of your manual searches online, and every request you make to Apple's Siri voice-controlled concierge on your iPhone.

A lot of the information that companies gather, particularly as they move to more real-time data gathering, ends up being "false positives." You send an e-mail that mentions this or that, or make an online purchase of a baby gift for a pregnant friend. The next thing you know, you are being shown stuff only a parent would want to buy. But you're not a parent, and this annoys you. If you're a member of Gen D, it more than annoys you. It makes you *hate* the seller and the online site that provided the information to that seller. Maybe you drop the service that got the whole thing started. Perhaps you blog about it. Perhaps you even join a boycott with others who've had the same experience. Gen D members may set out specifically to exact revenge. Your business might as well be dead.

If you remain unconvinced that this is a very serious problem, consider one more cautionary, true tale of Big Data.

Every time you go shopping, you share intimate details about your consumption patterns with retailers. And many of those retailers are studying those details to figure out what you like, what you need, and which coupons are most likely to make you happy. Target, for example, has figured out how to data mine its way into your womb, to figure out whether you have a baby on the way long before you need to start buying diapers.[8]

You may have heard about this, or if not, can figure out where it's going. You may be surprised at just how serious this really is.

It turns out that Target assigns all online customers "Guest ID numbers" that are linked to their names, credit cards, e-mail addresses, and so on, and then associates those numbers with a history of every purchase and any demographic information Target is able to collect or has purchased from other sources. Over time, Target's data analysts figured out a set of products that they believed to hint strongly that a customer was soon to have a baby (certain kinds of soaps, extra-large bags of cotton balls, and so on).

When Target sent a book of coupons for baby-related items to a teenager in the Minneapolis area, her father hit the roof and confronted a store manager. He later found out, from a talk with his daughter, that she was pregnant. Target's response to this fiasco was to change how it sends the coupons to make it less obvious.

Now, think about everything you now know about Gen C and especially Gen D. Consider this Target story. And look at what Andrew Pole, who developed Target's pregnancy prediction model, told the *New York Times* for a story about data mining and the pregnant teen in Minneapolis.

How are women going to react when they figure out how much Target knows?

"If we send someone a catalog and say, 'Congratulations on your first child!' and they've never told us they're pregnant, that's going to make some people uncomfortable," Pole told me. "We are very conservative about compliance with all privacy laws. But even if you're following the law, you can do things where people get queasy."[9]

Queasy, indeed! This is one of the more egregious examples of the 360-degree view reliance on data. In this example, there were probably multiple generations of customers—Gen C, Gen D, and even older customers—who, *at best*, ended up being very suspicious of Target. The Target story is a tale of 360 run amok.

Getting beyond Data

In a nutshell, the big challenge going forward is to find a way to use data that makes sense, especially as the sheer amount of data accumulated becomes so large it needs a name that hasn't even been invented yet. That is the alternative to being killed by data or committing suicide. It needs to be done in a way that does not violate customers and potential customers, does not force behaviors on them that they will reject, and creates a kind of authenticity that allows for the all-important sense of discovery we have described. You have to demonstrate to Gen D that if you're going to use their data—data they expect you to have but do not really want to know you have—you are not going to disrespect them. You have to provide them with the opportunity to discover something so awesome that their attention doesn't shift to the reality that you are tracking, mining, analyzing, and so on—in other words, so they don't spend any time thinking about the fact that you *are* managing someone who does not want to be known as your customer or be in anything that might be called a relationship with you.

But that is only part of the solution. Data alone is not going to keep you from the fate that awaits in the customerpocalypse. Data tells you about the customer's past, but what about the customer's future, especially that customer's future with your business? What good is data that tells you *who* your customers are if you do not know how to turn that into the right actions?

If you are viewing your Gen C and Gen D customers only through the lens of data, you are looking at the equivalent of an old, fuzzy, black-and-white TV. You are not going to see them in the colors that can reveal a deeper understanding and that can guide you to do what's best.

3

ADDING JUDGMENT AND DESIRE

Source: Barton Silverman/The New York Times/Redux. Used with permission.

Your business now has vastly more customer information than ever before. This information is no longer restricted to your internal customer database, but is complemented and frequently dwarfed by syndicated market research, sentiment, and opinion inferred from voice and text analysis, and perhaps even data aggregated from social media and Websites. It's that latter category of aggregated data from social media and Websites that is such a game changer, particularly when it comes to Gen D. People are no longer surprised to find that you can get information about employees from LinkedIn that is richer than anything their own human resources departments have on hand. Now this detailed information can be correlated from across many domains—a source of even more information, or the collective memory of interactions from across the Internet.

It is only useful, though, if you can figure out how to complement it. Sure, data can tell you *who* the customer was, but *who* is only one of the "six Ws" necessary to tell a full story. You'll see shortly why you need all six; they are no less important to great customer centricity than they are to top-notch journalism. Plus, data—that is, memory—can at best only *suggest* who your customer might be tomorrow, or who might be your next customer. You need to know *why* customers are interested in engaging in general and with you in particular. You need a clear picture of *what* you should be offering to particular customers, not just what you've already offered to the many other customers in your massive database. You have to identify *where* your customers, present and future, prefer to be served—across which channels, locations, and business jurisdictions. And you need to know *how* you are going to deliver what your customers expect, not just how you've done it before. This is the beginning of thinking in layers, a concept discussed in more detail later.

How do you get those other Ws? How do you go from the old black-and-white TV to color? It begins with putting the data in *context*. When data alone can be confusing and even toxic, and too much data can kill you, *context* is your first line of defense and the basis for actionable insight.

DATA IN CONTEXT

Chapter 2 describes data as a brain's memory. But to have memory only is to remain mired in the past, and to be largely ineffective. We cannot make decisions, and we can only replicate what has been done in the past without regard for new motivations or variation. Data, in and of itself, does not lead to good judgment. It cannot express or meet desire. When you combine memory with *intent*, data is put in context. Personality and individual interpretation are added to the mix.

Intent works bidirectionally, adding two dimensions to your view of the customer. First, *why* that customer comes to you (customer intentions) and second, *what* your own business wants to achieve with that customer (business intent). Intent expands who to who/ what/why. Customer desires and preferences—their intentions— represent a rich new vein of understanding that empowered organizations are learning to analyze and take seriously. While Gen D does not want to be sold to or "acquired" as one of your customers, they may well be willing to have a conversation with you. If you can get them to discover you so that you can listen and learn from their intentions, you will be in a much stronger position to connect and anticipate their preferences and continue the conversation. All information and no intention means the people in your business and the systems that support them become overwhelmed with too much wrongly structured information delivered at the inappropriate time and, more often than not, to the wrong place.

In short, *intent* comprises the personality of your customers, their goals, desires, needs, and preferences. It is also your interpretations of your customer, your business objectives, and how you want to engage with those customers. If data is memory, intent is *desire* moderated by *judgment*.

Only when you combine judgment and desire with memory can you begin to transcend the fuzzy black-and-white 360-degree data view. Intent transforms the black-and-white data to something rich in color. You go from "just the facts" to the color wheel. Intent makes data come alive, focused, and relevant. It transforms memory from simply knowledge of the past into part of a powerful knowledge tool for the present and future. It does this by transforming the reactive into the proactive. Think of data like Mount Rushmore, waiting to be worked by sculptors Gutzon and Lincoln Borglum. The sculpture of Washington, Jefferson, Roosevelt, and Lincoln they ultimately released from that massive rock was already there in the side of the mountain. Their intent released it.

FROM BLACK-AND-WHITE TO COLOR

A baseball analogy to star New York Yankees pitcher C.C. Sabathia helps describe this important concept of adding color and shows how much is lacking when you rely on data alone. It also illustrates how little value you get from relying on averages, as is typical with simplistic data analysis.

Sabathia throws his fastball about 40 percent of the time as his first pitch, followed by his slider (about 25 percent), his sinker, and then, rarely, his change-up. So, a batter just coming to the plate to face Sabathia is probably preparing for the fastball. What that batter is not doing is preparing for the average of all the pitches Sabathia is capable of throwing, because in this game you cannot prepare for an average. The average is as useful to that batter as calculating the average number of legs of barnyard animals on a farm with an equal number of cows and chickens. What good does it do you to know that average, which would be three?

How, then, does a batter make his judgment? Yes, he'll expect the fastball as the first pitch. But a major league hitter also looks at the pitcher's hands for a clue. He tries to home in on the seams of the ball

DATA
Who

INTENT
Why/What

as it leaves the pitcher's hands. Those are clues that begin to add a little bit of color to the data point *fastball*. Based on what the batter sees in those clues, he uses his judgment to makes adjustments.

As my colleague Dr. Rob Walker, who came up with this analogy, says about discerning these context variations, "Before you know it, you'll have a massive color palette to choose from," and a far better understanding of the customer's intent.

ADDING JUDGMENT TO THE MIX

With judgment added to the mix, data can be used to figure things out in a considerably more powerful way than looking at data alone. For instance, if you are a credit card company and one of your customers has two identical charges on his statement, the data alone really tells you nothing. But judgment allows you to determine that they may be duplicates, and your intent to have the best relationship with that customer may lead you to question one of the charges (using some rules, of course) before he even receives the statement for review.

Here is another example, one that may resonate directly with your own experience. Let's say you call your credit card company because you received your statement and there was what you think is a discrepancy. "I don't recognize this $70 charge for DBA/Scintilla Business Services," you tell the customer service rep. "What are you going to do about it?"

Lots of descriptions on credit card statements are cryptic, so this problem is common. If you had aggregated not only data of charges from Scintilla Business Services, but also information about other customers who have called about such charges, you could have your system use judgment. Was the charge removed for other customers? Was it removed only to have it reapplied by the merchant and then accepted by other customers? The data can show that, and your judgment can inform intent: What are you going to do when the issue comes up again. Perhaps you have information indicating that while it's an unfortunate name for a florist to use when running credit cards, nearly every customer who calls realizes during the conversation that he had sent flowers to his wife or girlfriend. Your system could aggregate the data, apply judgment, and over time learn something that allows you to fulfill the customer's intention to have this dealt with easily and clearly, all while meeting your business intent of having a seamless interaction with the customer that results in not having to undo a legitimate charge. You could even take it further, and recommend that merchant choose a better description for its business, or put additional prompting on such items on your Web-based statement to preclude the call in the first place.

All that adds *what* and *why* to the customer *who* provided by the data you keep in your business memory. Further, it lets you anticipate and respond optimally.

Another example is Farmers Insurance. Today, Farmers is well known for its strength as an insurer of personal and commercial properties. The company flexes its muscle and highlights this strength in its recent "University of Farmers" advertising campaign. Only a few years back, the executive leadership began to take a hard look at its business processes and spurred a transformation that took Farmers from a market follower to a market leader in some highly competitive market segments.

The company saw an opportunity in an underserved market for business owners' insurance, recognizing that insurance companies typically sell businesses on rather generic policies rather than policies that are unique to the specific needs of different types of businesses. Sure, Farmers could structure unique policies of that sort, but it meant that agents had to do a lot of back-and-forth both with systems and back-office underwriters to get the information they needed. It could take what seemed like forever, and potential customers would too often just end up underserved or with another carrier.

Perhaps you've opened a Brazilian barbecue restaurant, a churrascaria. Congratulations. You've got all your permits, you've hired staff, and you've installed your open-pit grill to roast the endless skewers of meat your customers will soon enjoy. You know meat, but you don't know how your open-flame grill will affect the expanded fire damage coverage on your first-ever commercial insurance policy, or whether your state allows for liquor liability coverage.

(Not all states do.) So, you call your Farmers agent, with whom you also have personal insurance.

It used to be that when you placed that call, your Farmers agent did not have that information at his fingertips. A Farmers agent knew houses and automobiles, but the complex thicket of rules associated with specialized small business commercial insurance was too much, too complex for quick offers and results.

So, you would have to wait for days and sometimes weeks for your agent to get back to you with a quote. It would take more and more time to underwrite and check the policy, and as the underwriters dug deeper into the specifics, you might have to start over. All that back-and-forth added to anxiety and delay. Instead of getting ready for your grand opening, you were dealing with your insurance company, because some of the things that are common in the underwriting of a restaurant specializing in Brazilian fare are quite different from the questions asked on the typical business insurance application. For instance, do you have an open flame? (Or, if you are opening a pizza joint, do you plan to send drivers out in cars to deliver to customers?)

Farmers knew there had to be a better way. The company worked outside-in from the customer experience and set as its goal a seamless experience for insurance agents and their customers. Farmers took customer intentions (give me a reliable quote quickly) and put all the data, those nasty business rules, and state and local regulations into context. Farmers wanted to ensure that its primary dedicated agents, as well as future adds of independent agents who can influence a customer to go with a particular insurance company, would all see the benefit of leading with Farmers.

Going beyond the data to get to intent doesn't have to be rocket science—it is about finding ways to incorporate the judgment and common sense of your most effective staff into all moments of truth with customers. Conceptually, Farmers Insurance made a very simple change to how it does business. It put itself in the shoes of its own agents and its customers and married data with intent. The company eliminated complexity. Farmers trained the system to remember to ask the right questions at the right time to make it easier to build a relationship with the business owner *and* get quotes quickly.

By organizing all the complex rules used to manage different types of risk, Farmers "wrapped and renewed" an unfriendly transaction system and transformed it into a customer-centric platform that captured its business intent and operationalized it. The transformation enabled thousands of agents, without specialized training, to deliver tailored policies for each kind of business. Intent made the difference. By combining what Farmers wanted and what customers wanted, Farmers went from the middle of the pack to revolutionizing its results in small commercial lines, doubling market share, and achieving a 70 percent increase in umbrella policy sales.

Oh, and by the way, the new approach slashed the typical two-week wait time for a quote to about 15 minutes.

I've seen businesses use intent, coupled with data, to increase their connection with customers. The turning point comes when they stop being slaves to data and to the impossible dream of being the hoarders of all data. After all, a common feature of hoarding is that eventually, no one at all—including the hoarder—can put a finger on a particular thing when it is needed. Instead, winners work incrementally to simplify the experience for customers and users by synthesizing intent from data and the dynamics of the interaction rather than just regurgitating more data than can be handled at moments of truth with clients.

How you handle moments of truth is critical enough now; in the customerpocalypse, it may be a matter of life and death. McKinsey & Company defines these moments as "those few interactions (for instance, a lost credit card, a canceled flight, a damaged piece of clothing, or investment advice) when customers invest a high amount of emotional energy in the outcome." And McKinsey goes on to state, "Superb handling of these moments requires an instinctive frontline response that puts the customer's emotional needs ahead of the company's and the employee's agendas."[1]

That is true, and when done right, those moments can be win/win for both you *and* the customer. Superb handling of these moments requires an intuitive engagement system that guides the frontline responses to address customers' immediate emotional needs in a way that ultimately serves the company's and the employees' agendas as well.

Bringing Smart to Big

Before we get to more examples of how leading organizations have married intent to data and information, it is important that you understand how we fell into data envy and what we need to do to get past it. While this might seem contrarian at a time when Big Data is touted as a panacea for what seems like everything from the common cold to the debt crisis, it's just not the case. Here's why.

When you rely on data alone, the only way to get smarter is to get more and more data, over and over. You have to be collecting data continually. And that data has to be cleaned and tested. A better way is to let go of the need to collect data for data's sake and instead get the right data, tested in a much more pragmatic and adaptive way than is typical. The scientific method points the way.

The scientific method has been around at least since the seventeenth century. But because marketers and other businesspeople tend to come from a different educational and training sphere than scientists and engineers, it's only recently that they've discovered the value of rigorous testing of hypotheses. This development has also been set back by the perspective that all you need is more data, and the truth will come forth.

What is the scientific method? According to *The Oxford English Dictionary*, it is "a method of procedure . . . consisting in systematic observation, measurement, and experiment, and the formulation, testing and modification of hypotheses." The scientific method has five steps. The first is *observation*, followed by *hypothesis, prediction, experimentation*, and *conclusion*. It's the approach scientists take to force themselves to state their proposed insights about what will happen, and only then let reality speak for itself.

That may seem difficult, but it's not. As the great English thinker Bertrand Russell once wrote, "Scientific method, although in its more refined forms it may seem complicated, is in essence remarkably simple. It consists in observing such facts as will enable the observer to discover general laws governing facts of the kind in question."[2]

Wouldn't you like to uncover not just a set of data correlations but truly understand the laws that really govern how best to engage with your customers?

The Power of Hypothesis

For our purposes, the key to understanding intent lies in taking an explicit step to propose the *hypothesis* regarding what data relationships may be causal rather than simple correlations. Exhaustive analysis of data can be misleading without an effort to propose and test which facts are the drivers that may be reliably related to predictable outcomes. Meanwhile, the data hoarders focus on accumulation, which, in turn, leads them into the trap of gathering more and more data. It is much better to look at just enough data to form a hypothesis and then *test the hypothesis*. In other words, apply the scientific method. Getting the data to help you uncover a customer's intentions is not only possible but—as it turns out—conceptually straightforward. It is as much about changing your mind-set as about anything else.

The counterargument to those who insist that Big Data promises the next great improvement in customer centricity is, again, that data—no matter how much you gather—simply cannot tell you what you need to know to transcend the 360-degree customer view. Data will not take your business to a higher level. Big Data is still data unwedded to intent.

More than that, the overfocus on data causes people to skip the hypothesis step, because it can be seductive to think that the data itself can deterministically drive particular conclusions. But in even modestly sophisticated settings, you cannot afford to do that. You still need to take the step of using the patterns you see as a basis to create hypotheses—and then for those hypotheses to be tested in ways sufficiently independent of the original data so you can really form and confirm the right judgments.

This change in mind-set doesn't come naturally to most people, as another example illustrates. In one company, there was a software team that had been trying to improve the performance of some key parts of the firm's information systems for a long time. But this team of a dozen or so bright, well-trained, talented software engineers kept missing its goal. So, the engineering manager brought in an expert in the scientific method to spend some time with the team to figure out why.

What was happening? The team had a singular focus to gather *data* to indicate where the performance gaps were coming from. But the problem—as is often the case in complicated settings—was that the results were inconsistent. Certain things would sometimes be really fast and then there would be periodic agonizing delays. The team looked at the data over and over to see whether it was "good" or "bad." They made changes to the system and then watched how the data in the system changed. They did all of this, however, without first creating testable hypotheses.

When the engineering manager talked with the team, no one said anything like, "Well, to improve performance, I think we need to understand how overall response time becomes surprisingly worse when there are more than a certain threshold of users from the service department"—suggesting interference between these two seemingly disparate aspects of the system. A working hypothesis like that could have been tested, and, whatever the conclusion, it would have provided insight into the root causes of the system behaviors.

The absence of a hypothesis only compounded their confusion, because each attempted improvement was just a shot in the dark absent a testable check on whether the data was actually indicative of the underlying laws governing the outcome. Each shot in the dark did nothing to contribute to the team's understanding of what was going on. They were just making changes, again and again, hoping that something would stick. Their work was the equivalent of randomly walking around a maze in the hope of finding the prize, without ever being able to identify which search strategies proved to be helpful or a waste of time.

What they needed was not more or better data. They needed to set out on a specific path, an *intentional* path, and see whether it got them to where they needed to be. And whenever they were surprised by a failed hypothesis, they needed to be able to use that failure as input to achieve some greater understanding, that is, to discern better how to improve the effectiveness of the next hypothesis.

Once the philosophy changed to create testable context that was validated to augment true understanding, the issues were quickly tamed. As the old Arabic proverb goes, "Experiment adds to knowledge; credulity leads to error." Believing you see patterns in the data without finding ways to validate is the difference between understanding correlation (these things go together) and understanding causality (when this happens, it is caused by a certain context married with my intent to achieve certain goals).

Hypotheses teach. If you are not testing, you end up just accepting what you think the data is telling you. Using intent as a means to develop and then test hypotheses allows you to project and anticipate future behavior. This creates knowledge that goes well beyond the 360 of the 360-degree customer view and can be extrapolated to (and tested on) other populations.

This chapter began by drawing the distinction between a brain that has only memory and one that combines memory with desire and judgment. Unfortunately, businesses settle for just the memory every single day. It is the basic model of customer service, of the misguided aspiration that a 360-degree customer view is all it takes. Businesses keep track of all their activities with customers, but they fail to discern what that information *really* means about what the customer wants and intends.

As the example of the software team illustrates, it's tough to get information systems people to solve this problem without a mindset change. Business folks end up resigning themselves to something along these lines: "Just dump out *all* the data, and I'll train my people to understand what we've got." The result is to doom the customer service staff, who will drown in the overwhelming deluge of noncontextual information.

NEXT-BEST-ACTION

How, then, do you work pragmatically with people in the context of numbing amounts of data, bringing judgment and responsiveness to the points of contact? An excellent example of how to apply the scientific method to integrate intent with the biggest data you can find is the concept of system-suggested *next-best-action*, which allows you to bring intent into the mix with customers at just the right time, in the right context, and without overwhelming whomever is engaging with your customer. It is a win-win for you and the customer.

Next-best-action works on the following premise: Offer and promote the right thing to the right person at the right time. It balances what your customer wants and needs and what your customer's interests might be with your own business objectives, and then continuously reevaluates and rebalances to optimize the outcomes. It comes close to the fly-fishing analogy mentioned earlier because it allows a certain subtlety to interactions. The next-best-action is carefully and thoughtfully constructed based on contextual information and insight.

This approach flips on its head the old-fashioned approach of creating a proposition for a product or service and then going out to find interest. By its very nature, the next-best-action approach provides the opportunity to be customer centric. Next-best-action is based on having the computer working along with the person or system, interacting with the customer across the range of applicable products—continuously optimizing, prompting the customer service rep to offer what really makes sense, or communicating with the customer directly in a manner similar to a self-service environment that just happens to always have the right options at hand.

A Customer Service Representative for one of the country's leading cable television providers tells a humorous story about just how "awesome" (his word) it can be when you marry data and intent to figure out the next-best-action, what a customer really ought to be offered, and then deliver it at the perfect moment in the interaction. One day, he took a call from a "nice old lady" who wanted to get cable television in her home. As he spoke to her, the top recommendation popped up on the screen: Offer her Cinemax.

Now, Cinemax is somewhat notorious for its late-night programming that features adult titles that have earned Cinemax the nickname "Skinemax," even in the mainstream media. The network itself even acknowledged the nickname when it used a play on the term to name its documentary series *Skin to the Max*.

"She reminds me of Grandma; she doesn't want Skinemax," the agent thought to himself. So he went through the call without making the recommendation.

Then, just as he was wrapping up, the woman said, "You know, there's this show on Cinemax that my friend was telling me about. Do you guys have Cinemax?"

Good for her—but the key to success is to make that same offer to those not bold enough to have asked for it themselves. In this case, the system was right and had suggested the exact right offer. I'll bet that service rep no longer ignores system recommendations.

The next-best-action, which can only be determined when data and intent have been combined and the information system is presenting what has been figured out in real time, is an approach that builds and strengthens your connections with customers. It goes well beyond the typical sales and buying experience to reshape the entire experience between customer and provider.

Pittsburgh-based PNC Financial Services Group provides a strong example of how next-best-action can enhance customer relationships. One of the largest companies of its kind in the United States, PNC provides retail and business banking, residential mortgages, wealth and asset management, and a host of specialized financial services for corporations and governments. It is a very competitive business.

PNC has a strong brand identity, but knew that the more compelling the customer experience, the stronger its brand would be. The context in large part is the big changes banks have been undergoing as more and more customers interact only online. Karen Larrimer, PNC's chief marketing officer, explained at the October 2013 Banking Analytics Symposium sponsored by *American Banker* magazine that PNC "has been moving from being product centric, with each product manager focused on pushing out his or her own products through the sales force, to customer centricity."

Banks, Larrimer noted, "Don't have the opportunity to interact with customers face to face as they used to. Only about 20 percent of customers use branches frequently, she estimates."[3] So the company set out to establish as the norm that its relationships with customers would always involve delivering relevant, personalized actions and offers in the right channel, at the right time, every time, even if those customers were never seen face to face. This had to be seamless to the customer to be a success. Achieving that success would mean PNC needed new kinds of insights into its customers that could be gleaned from customer data and marketing data but filtered with analytics that would ensure more than the conventional 360-degree customer view.

To reach its goal, PNC figured out that the main requirement would be the ability to coordinate all of its interactions with a given customer across all channels and in real time, so that each individual interaction would optimize the outcome for both the customer *and* the bank. And that would require a different approach to how it used technology.

The resulting system—PNC's Customer Interaction Management (CIM)—is a new "brain" for the bank that automatically analyzes customer data and the context of the inbound interaction, and then makes a next-best-action decision based on that data. The CIM brain functions as a centralized hub for managing all customer treatments across all channels, and works like a human brain in real time, automatically adjusting to match each situation, whether the situation involves a cross-sell, purchase of a new product, or a needed service.[4]

ADAPTIVE LEARNING

As PNC Bank found, next-best-action gives you a very good idea of what to do next with your customer. But it is only useful in that moment. To give it real long-term value, you need to combine it with *adaptive learning*. Together, these two tools form a virtuous circle that propels you beyond 360, because you are adding a second 360-degree view of intent. The result is a much broader, sharper perspective on the customer.

Adaptive learning is how you validate that the predictive analysis and hypotheses that led you to the next-best-action are still optimal. It employs advanced analytics to examine the trends and patterns across millions of customers to sense what customers would prefer, what choices would satisfy their needs, and how best to anticipate and predict customer behavior. The sheer volume of data allows for inferring customer intentions. By constantly testing new and different hypotheses, this approach can reveal patterns and probabilities that work with new Big Data and all the impure, not-quite-perfect data we already have.

Can a computer predict human behavior authoritatively 100 percent of the time? Of course not. But for customers whose behavior falls within certain parameters and patterns, I've seen the success ratio for using customer data and customer intentions to craft an upgrade offer or service recommendation climb to greater than 50 percent. More than half the time the customer says yes to the predictive suggestion framed as an offer.

For instance, let's say you want to explain some alternatives to a customer based on her expressed interests, data context, and your hypotheses about her receptivity to three appropriate products. Let's call them Product A, which customers with this context buy 80 percent of the time when offered; Product B, which customers buy 60 percent of the time when offered; and Product C, which customers buy 40 percent of the time offered. Typically, you'd suggest Product A first, since it's most likely to result in a sale. You'd offer Product B second, and Product C third.

What do you do if you suddenly find that Product A is now being accepted only 70 percent of the time, but Product C is now also being accepted 70 percent of the time? Would you simply keep Product A as the first offer and move Product C to be second? Reversing the order might tell you something useful. And going even further, to try and learn whether there is some correlation between what customers who are now favoring Product C had bought in the past could provide even more useful information. Indeed, perhaps changing circumstances now dictate that Product C should be your new champion—your best initial offer in this setting. Being able to challenge conventional expectations dynamically, finding new ways to apply all of that data coupled with intent, can help your organization learn and adapt. In many ways, adaptive change allows the computer itself to propose and test alternative patterns and hypotheses.

For PNC Bank's CIM system to succeed, adaptive learning was crucial. Next-best-action was simply not enough; the adaptive analytics are what ensure that the customer models being used to drive the customer treatment strategies stay relevant. The CIM brain learns on the fly and adjusts the models automatically so the bank never has to hurry to retool them manually whenever there are changes in customer behavior or market conditions. And because decisioning is managed centrally, the bank achieves a high level of consistency in those customer treatments throughout all the customer engagement processes that cross channels. If a PNC customer accepts an offer in one channel, CIM immediately removes the treatment from any other channel, so that there is no annoying duplication of the sort so despised by Gen C and Gen D—the kind that would make a customer question whether the bank was paying attention.

The adaptive learning built into the technology system allows PNC Bank to transition offers seamlessly from one channel to another, so a customer who visits an ATM might be offered a line of credit, with an option of getting more information sent to a smartphone or e-mail address. Important messages, such as fraud alerts, can be proactively sent to multiple channels chosen by the customer.

Organizing Your Insights

Bringing organized insight to the data teaches what to champion and what to challenge, so that you get real insights into fulfilling customer desires. Just as you are limited in how much you can learn from a single transaction, relying on data alone for learning is tremendously limiting. But add the data from transactions together, then subject that data to what you know about intent, and you not only find patterns but also get to test and refine those patterns. It is certainly not uncommon for customer behavior to change, and for what is popular and desired to change. If you want to be ahead of the curve and ahead of the trend, adaptive learning is the way to go. The more your business knows, and the better your ability to test new hypotheses, the easier it is to match your intent with your customers' intentions and use judgment to fulfill those desires in a way that mutually satisfies.

A great example of combining next-best-action and adaptive learning can be found in some of the divisions of the wireless provider Vodafone. With more than 400 million customers and 86,000 employees in 30 countries across five continents, Vodafone supports more than 14,000 stores around the world. The company's aggressive global growth comes at a time when the entire communications industry has felt its foundations shaken by new technologies such as voice-over-Internet and data-hungry smartphones as well as new opportunities that include mobile payments and streaming media.

A fact of life for today's communications service providers is the ease with which customers can switch providers and the simple fact that it is a much greater challenge (and cost) to win a new customer than retain an existing customer. There may be no better motivation for taking customer empowerment seriously and using every means possible to improve listening.

The connection between Vodafone and its customers' intentions is as strong as any I've seen. Every time a Vodafone pay-as-you-go customer reloads her phone, she receives a next-best-action "daily special"—a new, individualized offer to make her plan better that is based on her actual usage and what Vodafone has figured out will best serve the provider, the customer, and retaining that customer. The equation works like this: Take the objectives and intentions of the customer (the *who* and the *why*), add Vodafone's own aims and what the company wishes to and can accomplish (the *what*) given the customer's own intentions, and come up with an individually tailored deal that meets everyone's objectives. Then, to put icing on the cake, provision the deal immediately upon the customer saying yes.

Customers greet these offers with considerable enthusiasm. The acceptance rate for these offers is better than half. In other words, more than half the time when Vodafone customers reload their phones, they choose to take advantage of an offer from the provider.

All this done on such a regular basis may seem like a lot of work and tweaking for Vodafone and a lot of bother for customers, but it is actually what makes Vodafone the choice of hundreds of millions of mobile phone users. The entire basis of this rests on a merger of customer intentions and Vodafone's business intent, which Vodafone has figured out thanks to the company's deep understanding that its customers expect their objectives to be *known* by those with whom they do business.

For Gen D customers, the key to achieving such a high accept rate with offers will be for it *not* to feel like pursuit but their own discovery or that of a trusted friend. As Forrester Research's Peter Burris puts it, "Today's—and tomorrow's—customers can turn to each other to gather the information they need to make better choices in increasingly competitive markets. Using social, digital, and mobile technologies, they are learning new, more effective ways of engaging with brands. Customers are no longer dependent on passively awaiting offers—now they can more aggressively and inexpensively dictate their needs, both individually and in the aggregate . . . These empowered customers are pushing businesses into a new age, the age of the customer . . ."[5]

Still, even in today's Vodafone model, *everyone* benefits. The customer gets something that makes more sense for her, and Vodafone keeps her happy—and connected—without doing anything that doesn't also meet with the company's business objectives. The technology is only a tool, yet it is fundamental in moving from the engagement strategy to ongoing execution. The important lesson here is that Vodafone, as part of its customer retention strategy, chose to invest in listening first, learning what customers really want, and then proactively tailoring the company's response to match customer intentions.

Of course, Vodafone built customer processes to operationalize the marrying of memory with judgment and desire, of data and intent. As the company well knows, it is not enough just to have the right ideas about customer centricity; you have to be able to operationalize those ideas and execute on them.

One of the best things about how Vodafone fulfills desire is that the company does not need to have perfect data. It may seem counterintuitive, but getting away from perfection actually unleashes the capability to go beyond the restrictive 360 view. Those wedded to the old data-centric, 360-degree customer view spend inordinate time and energy working on and worrying about data perfection. This is unnecessary and actually hinders customer centricity. The corollary to data perfection is data completeness. If you are driven to perfection, you feel the need to capture every single piece of data lest you miss something that might be crucial. So, businesses are compelled to gather more and more and more, seemingly without end.

In an intent-led engagement with your customer, you need to let the rhythm of the interaction guide the offer. Things about the interaction itself—not just the analytics—have to figure into the equation. It's not just data, but "chemistry." Intent is judgment. The next-best-action may be a next question.

So, here's something worth asking yourself: How *little* data might you need to drive a successful, intent-led engagement with your customers?

FEEDBACK LOOPS

Adaptive learning becomes even more powerful and valuable when you incorporate feedback loops from the interaction with customers. This creates an opportunity for your intent to become smarter as the interactions evolve.

Information technology makes it possible for a system to infer things from the interaction, in real time. For instance, a customer who is filling out an online survey may suddenly slow down. It might be because of a distraction, but it might also be the result of a lack of decisiveness. The system can use that data, shift judgment, and possibly create an offer for the customer that takes into account those areas of indecisiveness.

In other words, the interaction itself provides situational data to the overall view of your customer. By seeing the dynamic of how the customer is responding and not responding you gain insights into the customer that you may have never before considered. That enhanced insight creates better alignment between your business and the intentions of your customers.

INTENT GOES BOTH WAYS

To keep aligned, the best exercise is to test your hypotheses against the reciprocity principle. We have long been told that having a 360-degree view of your customer data was the holy grail, but what we are now learning is that if you are to leverage intent to maximize your customer centricity, you also need to *give your customers a consistent view and experience of your business*. Intent goes both ways. Here's an example.

Consider a customer who has a significant small business relationship with his bank. He does a lot of business with the bank and there are a lot of transactions involving his business. The business uses many different services and technology solutions that the bank provides. This small business is a highly valued customer.

This same guy also maintains a personal checking account at the bank, one in which he doesn't usually keep a balance that comes anywhere close to the amount in his business account, which is in the tens of thousands of dollars.

One Monday night, when his balance in that personal account was $339.26, he wrote a check to his son for $350. The next morning, he went to the bank and deposited into his personal account a $200 check he had received in Monday's mail at home. That brought his balance to $539.26, but since the check he deposited was drawn on a different bank there was an overnight hold on making the funds available.

Tuesday afternoon, his son goes to the bank to cash the check Dad had given him. As a courtesy, the bank cashed it, despite the fact that the funds weren't available. But the system automatically spit out a charge for being overdrawn, and on Wednesday Dad receives a notice that he his personal account had been assessed $35 for the paid check.

Now ask yourself a question. This guy is a valued customer. His business account is important to the bank. Does it make sense for the bank to charge this outstanding small business customer a $35 overdraft fee on his personal account? Of course not. It makes no sense to him. And when he calls to complain, the service representative can only explain that the fee was appropriately charged according to the terms of his particular type of account. He could choose to pursue it with a manager, and most likely get it reversed. However, as is typical for a customer whose time is valuable, he does not choose to invest that extra effort, and instead is left with a bad taste in his mouth and an erosion of loyalty.

What that bank needed is what one global communications service provider (CSP) has begun to do to empower Customer Service Representatives. They are given a "budget for satisfaction" that corresponds to each customer. It is a rough dollar amount that can be "invested" with the customer during an interaction to make sure that customer is satisfied. It's up to the customer service reps to use it when they think it's necessary. So-and-so phoned in with a complaint?

Based on customer history and relationship, the company thinks his budget for satisfaction could to be up to $45, but the customer service rep thinks this time creating satisfaction will require a $15 credit. Go for it.

This global CSP is able to do this because of how the company is using information technology. With its old system, a customer might call in with an inquiry of the sort just described, and the rep would have to scroll through screen after screen to find any information relevant to addressing the customer's issue and coming to some resolution.

"You cannot imagine the number of screens the rep would see in the old way of doing things," explains the company's director of Customer Relationship Management. "In the new way, every-thing is contextual based on the reason the customer's calling in,"[6] which includes the customer's value to the company, past situations, the present issue, and the company's customer intent, and the business intent.

By streamlining and facilitating the interaction, the rep is given the opportunity to have a genuine conversation with the customer, to focus on the customer rather than on gathering data. No customer gets put on hold while the rep searches. This "means a more relevant interaction with the customer, and it means our customer interactions are more effective," says the director. "When you have a more relevant interaction with the customer, it becomes an opportunity for delight-ing the customer."

The ability to do this comes from using predictive analytics and the adaptive modeling it allows. "From a business user's standpoint—when you talk about the system being able to learn and adapt and get better and better, that's where it really hits home . . . We had these models before, but they can continuously improve, not every month or every six months or every quarter when we refresh them, but every time the call is over, the model has improved that much more."

In essence, what this global CSP is now doing is to pull in the subtle human skills and judgment of its service reps and let them determine the extent to which they think there is a need. All this happens while the company employs the system-driven judgment of next-best-action (to determine the budget) in conjunction with the dynamics of the human interaction to achieve a true optimization of the overall interaction. This is tremendously empowering for the Customer Service Representatives, while much more cost efficient for the company than designating what would end up being an unsatisfying average fixed amount to offer.

The ability to empower frontline staff with a budget for satisfaction requires a high level of institutional trust and good organization. Now think about how the bank is probably set up, channel-wise, and how the bank's systems probably work. The monthly fee for the personal checking account is generated automatically. The bank employees responsible for personal checking accounts are probably not the same people responsible for small business accounts. Do they talk to each other? Do their systems prompt them to think about the two accounts and how to handle them even if they are nominally responsible for only one? The systems surely have the data that tells them the customer has these two different accounts, but do the systems capture the business intent of the bank? Again, the sensible conclusion is that *he should not be charged that monthly maintenance fee* to begin with. But if he is, it is a powerful thing for the service staff to have a system guiding them that is based on the nuances of each particular customer relationship, and for them to know that they are empowered to offer remediation.

The bank needs to have that intent built into its decision framework, elevating the decision above a particular bubble of product-specific rules and data. If the bank hasn't figured out not to charge the customer, the customer has probably complained. If he has not complained, the explanation is likely either that he's not yet paying attention or he is quietly seething as he builds to a new level of frustration. Gen C customers will, over time, choose to get even by moving their business or letting some group of other potential clients know about their experiences with that bank. A Gen D customer would have set out to "destroy" the bank, not physically but certainly its reputation and brand.

How do you get intent linked to data and translate that into situational thinking? Just as you have a data repository representing organizational memory, you need to build an operational engine for business intent, encapsulating what your business wants to do, that is powered by information technology. You provide the synthesis of the data and the intent in each channel through which your customers engage, empowering the businesspeople to optimize each situation by allowing them to apply that insight to work directly, and in real time, to meet their needs. Forward-looking companies have turned around the way they deal with customers. They have made sure that their businesspeople who are engaged in service interactions with customers are armed with the best estimation of those customers' intentions. They provide enabling technologies that let their staff merge situational advice with their business judgment to keep customers connected and satisfied. All of this builds on the concepts of next-best-action and adaptive learning to provide customer service reps with answers to questions and with insights they might not have even thought of.

Remember the "financial supermarkets" discussed in Chapter 2? That business model failed because the banks were so busy gathering data and believing that all they needed to do was offer their customers the complete range of possible services to build a strong connection. But the banks failed to address how to make sure what they were doing captured their own business intent and exactly what their customers really wanted, in a way that could be effectively delivered by their staff.

OCBC Bank, a highly innovative Asian financial institution, has taken a different approach, one that has gotten the balance right by addressing customer intentions. When you enter a branch of OCBC Bank in Singapore to open an account, you are immediately given priority and paired with a highly professional customer service specialist, who takes you to a small enclave, comfortable and traditional. When the bank first rolled out its new approach, there were even professional greeters at the doors to escort new customers to these specialists.

In this special enclave, you sit side-by-side with the specialist and share a touch-screen computer with a swivel base mounted on the desk. The specialist asks about your financial planning and banking needs. As you chat, bank products pop up on the screen. Based on your profile and intent, only relevant and logical choices are offered because intent has focused the data and the interactions are continuously tuned based on how the interaction is unfolding in real time. You make some selections and are given advice, information, and guidance regarding what additional options are available. Only *after* you are comfortable with your selections does the system ask you for identification. Normal inside-out practice would insist on the identification first, but doing so after the customer is pleased with the service selections makes a big difference. The ID is scanned on a desktop scanner and the blanks in the forms are automatically filled in. The customer service specialist validates the information with you by showing it to you on the shared screen, and then the product selections on the screen become even more aligned with your needs. The system—now that it knows you—is thinking about what might be best. And what it thinks is completely, totally based on data and hypotheses about that data that have been tested in context, and are subject to continuous tuning by management. In one year, this revolutionary approach to customer engagement has moved OCBC to a clear number-one position in its Singapore market based on its "Net Promoter Score" (a concept explained in Chapter 6).[7]

A major component of OCBC's success is that when it comes to its technology systems, the company has begun to think in layers. Such thinking is the only way to get past the traditional legacy systems that hang like cement blocks chained to the legs of companies that may soon find themselves "swimming with the fishes." Those old systems are two-dimensional, but thinking in layers yields three-dimensional systems that address the variations in customers, variations in products, and variations in jurisdictions (which includes channels) that are common to nearly all businesses larger than mom and pop. Thinking in layers—sometimes called "inheritance" by computer technologists—is based on the idea of sharing everything that you can and only differentiating when it is necessary. Something in the system that describes how you do business in North America can be shared, and then broken out only if there are differences between the United States and Canada, and then only if there are differences between British

Columbia and Québec, and then only if there are differences between Montreal and Gaspé . . . and so on, all the while maintaining a single definition what is the same rather than having to reinvent the wheel each time. The same can be done with the attributes of a product: there are loans, for instance, and then there are specific types of loans that all share some of the same attributes and are different only in some respects.

Vodafone and OCBC are great examples of how powerful it can be when you think in layers, marrying data and intent and having the systems that can capitalize on that marriage. Now let's extend our C.C. Sabathia baseball analogy to this topic. Imagine you were able to marry data and intent in your head, with some kind of tiny software implant. You're facing C.C. Sabathia, and as you stand in the batter's box, the program is going through all the options, looking at all the colors, and whispering in your ear what the next pitch is likely to be. Your next-best-action will be better, and you'll see your batting average improve.

Perhaps baseball's not your game, and you are a chess player. There is a chess analogy that makes this point about combining human judgment with the power of computer analytics very well. Garry Kasparov is a former world chess champion whom many consider to be the greatest chess player of all time. In an essay reviewing a book about artificial intelligence,[8] he told numerous tales of playing against computers. In his own matches with technology, he was a consistent winner, even in his first effort against IBM's much touted behemoth computer Deep Blue. His victory against Deep Blue the first time turned to a loss in the rematch. Since IBM refused to have Deep Blue play a third match, we are left with an unsatisfying tie in this 1990s battle of man versus machine.

But thinking of how chess-playing computers might engage with and against human players continued to evolve. In 2005, Playchess .com—an online site—hosted a "freestyle" chess tournament. It was open to anyone, and teams could use computers. The prize money was considerable, and several groups of grandmasters working with several computers at the same time entered the competition.

Kasparov writes, "The surprise came at the conclusion of the event. The winner was revealed to be not a grandmaster with a state-of-the-art PC but a pair of amateur American chess players using three computers at the same time. Their skill at manipulating and 'coaching' their computers to look very deeply into positions effectively counteracted the superior chess understanding of their grandmaster opponents and the greater computational power of other participants. Weak human + machine + better process was superior to a strong computer alone and, more remarkably, superior to a strong human + machine + inferior process."

The same equations work in business with your customers. Writing about chess in the *International Herald Tribune*, Hartosh Singh Bal ended up making the case for next-best-action and adaptive learning in a much broader context. "So far, experiments with advanced chess suggest that the powers of man and machine combined don't just make for a stronger game than a man's alone; they also seem to make for a stronger game than a machine's alone. Allowing chess players the assistance of the best computer chess engine available during top tournaments would ensure that the contests really do showcase the very best chess being played on earth."[9]

How, in a business sense, do you capture the potential of that kind of tiny software implant when facing Sabathia on the mound, or the tremendous combined power of analytics and human judgment that wins chess matches? There is more to it than just data and intent. They are only two of three siblings.

In a customer relationship setting, unless the insight of next-best-action can be delivered to the right person having the conversation with your customer, it will forever remain an insight not actuated. What is happening behind the scenes of a seamless account opening at OCBC are activities that address all the accounting and regulatory requirements, funding the accounts, enabling PIN access, and issuing cards. In other words, there is *process* at work. It is a wholly new *customer-centric process*, and bringing it to life is something that all the data in the world could never do.

4

GETTING IT DONE
WITH CUSTOMER
PROCESSES

"Joe, these people say they want flesh-colored Band-Aids."

Source: © 1963 William O'Brian/The New Yorker Collection/The Cartoon Bank. Reproduced with permission.

We now have memory (data) together with judgment and desire (intent). Combined, they create wisdom that memory alone cannot provide. But something more is needed. To be responsive, to be able to respond with that wisdom, you need some muscle. Only with muscle can you put memory and intent to work and deliver results.

In the human body, skeletal muscles—also aptly known as "voluntary" muscles—have tendons that anchor them to bone and that are for locomotion. Processes, functioning as muscle, also have an anchor or foundation, found in the remaining three of the "six Ws" discussed in Chapters 2 and 3. Data is *who*. Intent expands the list to include *what* and *why*. Like tendons in muscles, working with the brain, processes work with data and intent to complete the list, adding *when* and *where* and *how*. Brains and brawn is better than brains alone.

Every human body depends on muscle. So, too, does your company. Muscle gives you agility, and when combined with brains you are capable of achieving a level of agility that is necessary to withstand the daily business exigencies. Consider "sense" to be data and intent and "respond" to be judgment (or decisions) and processes, and you can see what it takes to be agile and the situations you may find yourself in if you fail to be agile.

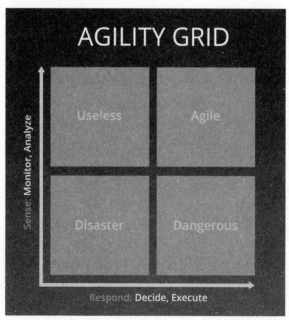

You certainly have processes by which you operationalize your company activities. To prepare for Gen D and the customerpocalypse, though, you need extra strong muscles. Your existing processes are not going to stand up to the onslaught. They don't even work the right way, because they do not have the extra strength that results from being imbued with a customer orientation. You need *customer processes*.

Customer processes are what allow you to look in from your customer's perspective at your business to see it as a whole—across channels, silos, and whatever else breaks up your company into parts that potentially present a disconnected, disjointed experience to the customer. Seeing the whole from the customer-in perspective is a prerequisite to giving customers a seamless, coherent experience of doing business with you.

When your processes are *customer* processes, you eliminate the tendency to respond without sensing. Processes that are not customer processes function without the sense part of the earlier analogy; their responses do not lead to good results. In the United Kingdom, the giant Tesco grocery chain is learning this the hard way. The second-largest retailer in the world after Walmart as measured by profits, and after Walmart and Carrefour the third-largest as measured by revenues, Tesco was "once the big beast of British business." But it responded to competitors Sainsbury's and Waitrose by trying to go upmarket, and now at least one British stock analyst claims that "Tesco is losing customers to everyone."[1]

The big shift Tesco made in its business model was possible because of its muscle, but that muscle does not seem to have been employed with a good sense of customer intent, which is part of the brains. In other words, Tesco fell into the "dangerous" part of the Agility Grid because the company responded without sensing what its market really needed and what its customers really wanted.

Then there's the example of Google. In May 2012, Google announced that it had acquired Motorola Mobility, which would enable the company "to supercharge the Android ecosystem" and "enhance competition in mobile computing."[2] The purchase price: $12.5 billion.

Google's logic behind its purchasing decision was the sense that users of its Android operating system wanted more integrated solutions like the ones offered by Apple, and that the company could gain a competitive advantage if it could get into the device business and control not only the software side of the equation, as it already did, but the hardware side as well.

That logic, however, was fatally flawed. Google's sense of its customers was incomplete, and hence incorrect. In between the end users of smartphones that run the Android system are Google's *real* customers for Android—other manufacturers of smartphones. That is one of Google's critical channels.

What Google did in response to this incomplete sensing was to execute a defective response that disenfranchised that critical channel, encouraging dissent among a large and important customer base. The $12.5 billion is the worst high-profile investment thus far in this decade.

The only good news in this story is that Google figured out it had made a mistake and responded agilely. In late January 2014, the company announced it would unload Motorola Mobility on Chinese electronics maker Lenovo Group for $2.91 billion. That's a lot of lost cash, but Google can afford to make a multi-billion dollar mistake now and again . . . at least for now. Some analysts have argued that calculations of the full scope of the deal and what had transpired in the short time Google owned Motorola Mobility make what seems like a $9.5 billion hit far less significant.[3]

But the key was being able to sense the error and respond in time. This supports Google's reputation as a company that, from this perspective, gets Gen D.

Success on the Agility Grid can be achieved only by embracing an outside-in way of thinking. "In the age of the customer, customers activate your business capabilities, lighting up the people, processes, and technologies that constitute your corporation. Thus, the outside-in approach to reinventing your business requires understanding how your customers activate your capabilities and what types of customer experiences will enable you to win and translating that knowledge into investments in business technology that will systematically give you a market advantage."[4] Thinking outside-in about the processes that help you run your business gets you to processes that can map a customer's intention with customer information to drive and guide a customer engagement to a completion that corresponds to what both you and your customer want.

Gen C expects nothing less; they want what they want, and they want to know you work to give them what they want. Gen D's expectations are even greater, yet ever more subtle. They want what they want, and you had better give it to them seamlessly, without a hint that they are being sold to or managed. Otherwise, they've "gotcha." And they will make sure the world knows about it.

THE BEST EXECUTION FOR EVERY CUSTOMER INTERACTION

To achieve seamless customer interactions you must have customer processes that make customers experience your business in a way that is personalized, and that the customer senses is unique to his or her individual situation. No process can make that possible unless it is a customer process that fuses data and intent with the ability to execute.

This is where the customer process needs to be especially intelligent and work particularly fast. A customer process worthy of the name needs to be able to change to meet the particulars of any given customer, on any given day, with a unique payload of specific and even one-time requests. Yet no single aspect of the troika of data, intent, and process, nor even two of the three, can deliver what is needed. It is only when memory, intent, and muscle *work as one* that you can achieve effective customer-centric outcomes.

As discussed in Chapter 3, Farmers Insurance and Vodafone leveraged insight into their own procedures and customers within new customer-oriented processes that put those insights to work. Farmers is a good example of reversing the inside-out thinking that characterizes traditional business processes—one process for sales and another for underwriting, for example—and embracing the outside-in model. Vodafone uses the rich breadth and depth of information to analyze probability and infer customer intentions, and then creates a brand-new customer process that wins loyalty in an intensely competitive marketplace.

The Customer Interaction Management (CIM) system "brain" created by PNC Bank (described in Chapter 3) paid off with customers, too, delivering a positive lift in revenue to the company from the first day it was rolled out. Since then, it has driven exceptional levels of customer satisfaction—a sure sign of more authentic customer engagement in these times. Temkin Ratings now rates PNC as number one in customer experience among banks in the northeastern United States and second nationally, behind only credit unions.[5] In addition, PNC is the only U.S. bank to receive an "A" in online marketing and promotion from Bank Monitor.[6]

CIM has been equally popular with PNC's Customer Service Representatives, because the system prompts them with relevant offers and guides them through the process when they are interacting with customers—eliminating the need to ask a lot of questions to gauge the potential for cross-sell and upsell opportunities. CIM "has helped call center agents know what to say next to a customer on the phone."[7]

PNC "already makes available a million offer decisions a day in customer interactions through all major channels."

In these examples, customers are already in the door and engaged to a greater or lesser degree. What about initial interactions with customers?

FIRST IMPRESSIONS

Everyone knows the adage that you never get a second chance to make a first impression. These are words businesses ought to live by. To illustrate their importance, let's again use a bank as an example.

Today's banks are burdened by their past. Take a look at the old-fashioned ways so many banks inflict on their customers just to open an account. Manual forms and multiple identity checks create delays and inconvenience. For a Gen C depositor, such a combination is a deadly combination, and by the time Gen D members become a big percentage of bank customers, it will be too late for those that haven't adapted. Gen D may hardly ever even enter an actual brick-and-mortar bank. No wonder customer-focused account opening is becoming a litmus test for whether a bank will be able to compete.

BB&T Corp. chose to face this challenge head on, though in a different way than OCBC approached an analogous challenge in the earlier example. The bank, founded in 1872, is one of the top 15 in the United States. It has a big footprint in the country, with 1,800 banking centers in 12 states and more than 30,000 employees. Like most other banks, BB&T had long employed the traditional approach to welcoming a new customer, one that had evolved over decades. A person had to come into the bank and fill out a lot of forms, and then those forms would be sent to people in the back office. Customers would wait while signature cards were filed, identities were verified, and funds were finally put into the new account. After 9/11 and enactment of the PATRIOT Act, things were made even more cumbersome. One section of the act requires a more stringent "Customer Identification Program" with a larger number of documents to check. And more recent regulations have continued to make such processes increasingly onerous for both banks and clients.

For banks that do things this way, like BB&T used to do, new-fangled channels for signing up new customers, such as the Internet or over the telephone, do not make things faster or easier. These channels all rely on the same old steps. At some point, the same humans in the back office are engaged and the same paper forms are required. If anything, the introduction of new channels only complicates the situation. The traditional processes saw to it that BB&T simply could not capitalize on the potential of newer channels to optimize the customer experience, generate new revenue, and lower the costs that come with having people sitting in branch offices waiting for new accounts to walk in the door.

Still, as BB&T watched its competition introduce online account opening, the bank needed to do something. So, BB&T's information technology people worked feverishly to create an online account opening facility comparable to that of its competitors, as quickly as possible. They ended up slapping something onto the bank's Website that was, of course, the same old process, but with a Web face. The results were not what the bank's executives expected—more often than not, the online applications were abandoned.

The lesson here is that simply adding a new channel does not fix underlying problems. The fact that the legacy processes were difficult and unfriendly was only part of what BB&T was confronting. While the Web solution allowed customers to do the digital equivalent of filling out all the forms needed to open an account, BB&T found that the bank could not meet the commitment it spelled out to online customers that their accounts would actually be opened in a timely manner and with little effort. Plus, if a customer abandoned the online account application midway through filling it out but then wanted to talk to someone on the phone or go into a branch, that customer had to start all over. There was no sharing whatsoever of what a customer did across these multiple channels.

There is another important lesson here: Don't bake too much into a given venue. Intent has a certain logic that needs to be provided to the customer as a whole. You want to reach into each channel or venue where the process needs to be accessible, but you do not want to lock processes into specific channels by making them, in a sense, part of each different channel's unique system's code.

The BB&T situation was bad enough for customers in general. For Gen C customers, the ones most interested in such online interaction, it spelled anger and frustration. BB&T had to fix things fast. Soon enough, Gen D will be needing banks, too. For the fix, the bank set out to do things differently. BB&T designed a new account-opening process that not only automated all of the back-office procedures whenever possible, but also *unified* these procedures with their customer-facing front-office processes. These included the processes associated with walking into a branch and dealing with a Customer Service Representative. By unifying the front-office requests for service across channels with the fulfillment of those requests in the back office, BB&T eliminated delay and errors and improved the experience for all involved.

BB&T figured out how to bring the right decision to the right place, and succeeded in providing a consistent and streamlined experience— not just a process, but a *customer process*. It no longer matters whether the customer goes to the BB&T Website to open an account, phones into a call center, or walks into a branch. Each channel works consistently. And staff at call centers can now pick up so-called abandoned applications from a self-service channel. In other words, if you are on the BB&T Website and begin to apply for a new account but then stop before completion, you can phone the bank later and talk to someone who can restart the process right where you left off.

SEAMLESS CUSTOMER PROCESSES

Gen C customers expect just this kind of seamlessness. Gen D customers *do not* expect it, but that is only because they are not really conscious of seamlessness unless you fail to give it to them. The bottom line is that Gen D cannot really conceive of things being any other way.

Using business rules to carry intent into the process, BB&T automated key functions such as ID verification, credit scoring, and credit decisions to approve, reject, or refer the application for further review. Additional areas of automation included real-time interfaces, monitoring of funding, back-end system updates, and confirmation e-mails.

The results have been extremely positive. Application abandonment has decreased by half. Operational costs associated with support staff have dropped by 75 percent, because so many manual tasks are no longer needed. The time it takes to open a new account, which in some cases used to be as much as two weeks, is now just minutes. Some 90 percent of customers reported being "very satisfied" or "satisfied" with their account-opening experience with BB&T. BB&T customers no longer have to wonder why the bank has the kinds of problems that they would never, ever consider to be valid ones to have in the first place.

The solution turned into a significant amount of new business as well. One of BB&T's executive vice presidents likens it to what the bank would have brought in if it had 75 or so additional, mature brick-and-mortar branches. Just opening that many new branches would have cost upwards of $500 million, but BB&T realized the value at a fraction of the cost.

For BB&T, helping their customers navigate this new channel was an opportunity to bring their customers into sharper view. The bank had invested in a 360-degree customer data view, but the initial experience trying to go online had demonstrated that, at minimum, BB&T needed better interaction between its staff, systems, content, and business rules. That pointed to needing another 360—*intent*, and a final 360 of *process*. If it could automate some functions, BB&T believed it would achieve greater efficiency that would benefit customers. But beyond this, BB&T realized that its siloed information and process was hindering true customer engagement.

Only when BB&T addressed these problems and developed the new approach did the bank succeed. Success came from imagining its processes from the customer perspective and modeling service according to what customer processes would look like. BB&T added process muscle to its memory and its judgment. Adding yet another 360 was the key to bringing BB&T customers into a relationship driven by data, intent, and process.

From a customer perspective, channels are simply choices, and customers expect the freedom to move seamlessly from one channel to the next. Why not? They can start watching a movie on the television, pause, and then resume watching on a tablet or laptop computer. They can stream their music libraries from personal cloud storage at Amazon or Apple to their mobile phones and home entertainment systems. Why can't they have the same seamless experience with their banks?

To be fair, it is far more difficult to accomplish seamlessness of that sort in a business such as BB&T. Changing the channel changes the experience, and there are a lot of internal things the bank must address. You need to be able to leverage the 85 percent or so of the customer experience that should be cross-channel, and make that work across channels, while also being able to perfect the venue-specific part of the experience that makes the relationship stick. In the end, however, none of this matters to the customer. Customers do not really care that you have to have that capability. For the most part, customers have little or no interest in hearing that you are living up to their expectations, or how. They just want their expectations met. Period.

Meeting customer expectations—and their genuine expectations, the ones that really matter most to them—*must* be front and center if you are to survive the Gen D customerpocalypse. Two researchers have put it well:

> Digital marketing is about to enter more challenging territory. Building on the vast increase in consumer power brought on by the digital age, marketing is headed toward being on-demand—not just always "on," but also always relevant, responsive to the consumer's desire for marketing that cuts through the noise with pinpoint delivery.
>
> What's fueling on-demand marketing is the continued, symbiotic evolution of technology and consumer expectations. Already, search technologies have made product information ubiquitous; social media encourages consumers to share, compare, and rate experiences; and mobile devices add a "wherever" dimension to the digital environment. Executives encounter this empowerment daily when, for example, cable customers push for video programming on any device at any time or travelers expect a few taps on a smartphone app to deliver a full complement of airline services.[2]

GETTING BEYOND BUSINESS PROCESS MODELING

How do you meet these changing customer expectations in the context of process? What is the starting point for creating genuine customer processes?

Just as businesses focus on data for the sake of data, just as they miss intent time and again, businesses also tend to impose broken, inside-out processes on their customers. Even the best of these, the ones that make customer experiences better than their competitors, are more about the business than the customer. Few businesses rethink their processes completely from the customer perspective. Such is the classic problem of business process modeling, which tends to document the existing series of *internal* steps in a business line or function or channel. And what happens when there's a new channel? More often than not, those internal steps are simply

replicated, creating an additional silo to foster disconnected customer engagement.

How do you avoid the trap of traditional business process modeling? To put your customer into sharper view, you need to begin thinking about processes, and continue to think about them, with one
question in the forefront: How does my customer want to engage with
me? Start there, and you will never make the mistake of *not* assum-
ing that your customers will naturally want to be able to move from
a social media interaction (e.g., a rant or rave on Twitter) to an online
chat, to a call center engagement, to a visit to a physical retail location.

This is not to say that you should ignore your channels, but rather
that you must design in ways that unify how they work for your
customers. Right now, mobile and social channels are the big news.
Indeed, they are powerful and disruptive. But they cannot be hived
off within your larger enterprise. They must not be constructed as
silos, somehow exempt from everything else and doing things their
own way. Your perspective needs to be that they are just another way
customers deal with your company, because that is how customers see
them. And they have to be invisible as channels, because that is how
Gen D will (not) see them.

Once you're there, you can begin to design customer processes that
put data and intent to work together.

Where do the obstacles lie? Peter Burris writes, "The challenge of
systematically understanding and serving customers derives from the
fact that increasingly customers enjoy the freedom to take whatever
journey suits their perceived need. Efforts to tighten down process
models for engaging customers ultimately are frustrated by the complexity of empowered customer scenarios and choices: When customers are on the other end of engagement, are free to move around, and
hold market power, you cannot design and implement a successful
end-to-end engagement process."[3]

True, if you are stuck in the rut of using technology in the traditional ways. The good news, though, is that technology is fully capable of adapting to allow you to manage *real-time engagement at a
process level*. Most technologists say otherwise, because of the way they
think . . . not because of the technology itself.

CROSSING LINES

For Prudential Group Insurance, part of one of the world's largest financial services institutions with operations in the United States, Asia, Europe, and Latin America, multiple lines of business spelled problems for customer service. The company did not know how to handle things if a client crossed those lines. So, Prudential set out to fix things by designing the customer process from the perspective of a client specifically needing to cross lines of business as a matter of course.

Just how difficult did the old way make things for Prudential clients when they contacted their insurance provider with a new request? The company itself said that multiple silos of information translated into "an inconsistent service experience" for clients. Data was housed in eight separate silos. Staff who dealt with customers were in multiple call centers, and it was impossible to get a comprehensive view of a client or an effective way to engage with them. More important, it was impossible for clients to get a comprehensive view of Prudential; they could readily see that the experience was fractured. It could take eight different systems just to service one customer, and Prudential had long needed to staff at excessively high levels just to achieve an adequate level of customer service at peak times. A lot of Customer Service Representatives were sitting around much of the rest of the time.

A central issue was that the business had been built through acquisition, often with multiple systems being maintained, and this was putting a burden on the staff to integrate user experiences that crossed systems. Prudential set out to fix this problem by building new customer processes that mapped information and data to customer intentions and drove customer service according to those specific intentions. What they wanted was a consistent service process that worked the same way no matter how a customer tried to reach Prudential. What they created was a customer process that allowed *any* customer service associate to deal with *any* call for *any* product. That is precisely what customers increasingly expect—an experience in which whatever the person on the other end of the phone might be using triggers the right questions, gathers the right answers, and integrates everything together.

Similarly, American Express has put its customers in sharper view with a customer service revolution within its World Service organization. The company had long positioned the American Express brand around the actual card and the benefits that come with being an American Express member. But with the move to more and more online transactions, the inevitable march of alternative payment mechanisms, the company found that traditional use of the physical card was under threat. Given that reality, how could American Express retain a customer base that had been built around having that piece of plastic in your wallet, expand to capture Gen C customers and grow to engage Gen D? After all, Gen D will reach a station in life where it might make sense to discover American Express, and when that happens every Gen D member will have brought along all the characteristics that make them so uniquely desirable, and dangerous, for any business to engage.

American Express realized that the true benefit membership provides to its customers is not in the card itself, but a relationship galvanized by trust and an extraordinary level of service and attention backing up the card. So, the company decided to deepen relationships with customers as a key strategic imperative. It began by fostering a culture of excellence in the service staff—replacing the traditional "Customer Service Representative" title with that of "Customer Care Professional." This was much more than a name change, reinforced by hiring standards, training, and by empowering these Customer Care Professionals with levels of flexibility to deliver even more outstanding service. This meant creating an integrated global network of 16,000 Customer Care Professionals across nearly two dozen servicing locations, all focused on a relationship-driven approach to customer service.

This approach relies on active listening and creating an emotional connection with customers. American Express uses customer feedback as its primary measure of success—specifically, how likely are American Express members to refer or recommend the company to their friends and colleagues. This intense focus on customer relationships has provided American Express with a loyal following of brand ambassadors that has helped the company earn seven consecutive

J.D. Power & Associates awards for highest customer satisfaction among U.S. card companies, as well as numerous other international customer service awards.

How did American Express get there? The company realized it could create better value for itself by providing greater value for its members, and that getting service right would provide a true competitive advantage. Research shows that consumers willingly spend considerably more with companies that provide great service. Surveys also show that vast numbers of consumers have stopped transactions due to subpar service. American Express knew that if it could create a more intimate relationship with its customers, it would provide greater opportunities for the company.

American Express thought about its billions of customer interactions and how they could be dealt with in a different, better way. How could the company combine data, intent, and process to differentiate itself? American Express wanted to use these elements not only to meet, but *exceed* the expectations of its members.

Customer expectations are informed by broadening service experiences across industries through multiple touch points, something American Express already knew, and that more informed consumers now share their experiences via social media. Consumers are in a very strong position of influence because of the viral nature of social media and the 24/7 access to information that mobile computing enables. The connections members make in their personal lives and via social media create opportunity for American Express.

All of this meant that American Express needed to embrace a new service paradigm and, in fact, change at American Express was driven through the service organization and managed upward. The company asked itself how it could make a positive impact in the lives of American Express members. If American Express was in the business of serving its customers, then that meant the company could no longer view interactions with customers as transactions that required reducing average handling times in order to get clients off the phone quickly. Because every customer interaction was unique, American Express needed to empower its Customer Care Professionals to deliver on the promise of personalized care to its members. This was the only way American Express could overcome the preconceived notions members had regarding its customer service and deliver an experience that exceeded customer expectations.

This involved a philosophical shift from transaction servicing to what came to be known as Relationship Care, which recognizes that the company is in the relationship business and needs to deliver a human connection. Knowing that great brands are built upon emotion, the core mission at American Express was refocused on being the most respected service brand in the world with Relationship Care enabling, engaging, and empowering its Customer Care Professionals to deliver on that promise.

BB&T, Prudential, and American Express all accepted the challenge of creating customer processes. They married data and intent and put them both to work in service of an outside-in customer process rather than an inside-out business process. This is the most difficult task and has nothing to do with technology and everything to do with mind-set. Old habits die hard. It is human nature to want to continue to project your traditional world view.

Getting to the point where you can actually deliver the best possible customer process is easier said than done. You need to look past the immediate engagement or transaction and imagine that your customer will be with you for a long time, even a lifetime. How will that journey change over time? How will your customer want to interact and engage with you at different points in that relationship journey? You will need to tailor your customer processes so they are adaptable to any situation that might arise.

The ability to adapt processes to any situation is critical to the survival of companies. Today, that may be no more apparent than in the U.S. health care industry, which is undergoing significant changes due to the Affordable Care Act and other legislation and regulations. For instance, many health care companies confront a radical overturning of their traditional business models, finding themselves having to interact directly with consumers where they once dealt primarily with employers. These new interactions focus on patient care and overall care management. As a result, health care providers of all sorts have been forced to become more customer-focused, and quickly.

That was the very situation faced by Telerx, a business process outsourcer (BPO) and subsidiary of the pharmaceutical giant Merck that is trusted to do critical work for other firms. Many other top pharmaceutical companies outsource critical operations to Telerx, including multichannel customer engagement. Through its 14 traditional and emerging contact channels, Telerx interacts with millions of customers, consumers, patients, and health care providers every year. In addition to needing an "audit-proven" solution to address regularly evolving federal regulations, Telerx was being barraged with changing customer requirements and demands for enhanced multichannel contact capabilities from its client's customers. The technology in place was built around cumbersome contact center solutions that required too many one-off changes, making it very costly to keep pace with all these demands. The technology, difficult to automate and standardize across clients, could simply not keep pace with the company's business processes as they grew exponentially more complex.

Telerx needed a way to tailor its processes to manage this growing complexity. The solution also needed to position Telerx to provide higher value-added services to an expanding customer base that was converting the company from a traditional contact center service provider to a provider of business advisory services. *Adaptability* was indeed at the center of what Telerx needed to accomplish.

Ultimately, because the company embraced the concept of outside-in customer processes, Telerx was able to bring its technological systems up to speed. The solution combines a business rules engine with business process management, providing a great example of using the cloud to deliver quick implementations with an understanding that ongoing improvement of intent and process would deliver the full benefit. It provides strong case management and automated workflow capabilities. And, so important in the health care industry, the solution meets or exceeds all audit and security requirements, and it ensures easy integration with internal data center systems, third-party applications, and client systems.

With its new customer processes, supported by digital technology, Telerx has *built for change*—with customers at the very center of everything.

BUILDING FOR CHANGE

Even if you do embrace the idea of overturning your inside-out processes and replacing the way you do business with outside-in *customer processes*, you still have work to do. Just as muscles atrophy so, too, customer processes can deteriorate. And just because you may have figured out how to combine the 360 degrees of data, the 360 degrees of intent, and the 360 degrees of process, the muscle memory it brings you and which serves top-tier athletes so well, is not going to serve you very long. In fact, it won't give you any sort of advantage the very next time a customer engages with you in a way that does not correspond to something you have already experienced. It could be the very next day after rolling out your new customer process.

Muscle memory is what allows you to replicate everyday activities that become automatic. But more than that, it is what makes those automatic actions improve with practice. Think of riding a bicycle or touch-typing on a keyboard. For top-tier athletes, muscle memory is what separates your ability to serve reasonably well in a friendly tennis game and their ability to put a serve right on the line, time after time.

Patterns are part of that memory, and knowing those patterns definitely is powerful. But with your customers, muscle memory is detrimental if it is so based on patterns that your customer process—though better than a traditional business process—ends up getting stuck in a repetitive, unadaptive framework.

To avoid such a situation, a customer process must be more than seamless. It must be built to be dynamic, able to shift how it works according to any particular customer situation or circumstance. How else can a customer process map to precise intentions?

In addition, your customers must experience a persistent connection. Customer processes cannot have disconnects or interruptions, and they must give the customer a consistent, unified view of your business. Making channels irrelevant to how the customer experiences your business is just as important as you having a single view of the customer.

Finally, a process that is not fluid and cannot evolve, is a process that does not simply become antiquated, but becomes a prison. Your business will change over time, perhaps over short periods. Your customers are evolving continually, perhaps even continuously if taken as a whole. The process must follow along with this evolution. Just as muscle memory needs to be retrained so the athlete can adapt to new situations, so, too, must customer processes be continuously recalibrated to ensure that they are working optimally.

This can be especially problematic in customer processes that are facilitated by traditional automation efforts. The long cycle times and unresponsiveness to new demands that characterize traditional automation efforts hamper the ability to bring intent and technical muscle to bear. Agility needs to be built into the technology for business users to trust that it will evolve to meet new demands, or those users will hopelessly fall back to manual procedures just to achieve the ability to change with the times—even if those manual procedures are doomed to disappoint.

Only when you have customer processes that actuate a seamless, dynamic, sticky (to use the Web slang for a site to which people return again and again), and evolvable way of doing business with your customer can you actually put data and intent to work in order to anticipate what customers will need, prefer, or want. The insights that come from next-best-action and knowing intent are useless unless they can actually change user experiences, adjust work priorities, assign specific tasks to individuals based on the situation, automatically launch new workflows based on context, and automate anything that makes sense.

There are four principles of customer process to keep in mind.

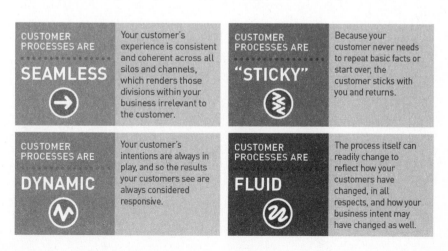

CUSTOMER PROCESSES ARE **SEAMLESS** → Your customer's experience is consistent and coherent across all silos and channels, which renders those divisions within your business irrelevant to the customer.

CUSTOMER PROCESSES ARE **"STICKY"** Because your customer never needs to repeat basic facts or start over, the customer sticks with you and returns.

CUSTOMER PROCESSES ARE **DYNAMIC** Your customer's intentions are always in play, and so the results your customers see are always considered responsive.

CUSTOMER PROCESSES ARE **FLUID** The process itself can readily change to reflect how your customers have changed, in all respects, and how your business intent may have changed as well.

This is how you transcend the limited customer view that is all about data, add the dimension of intent, and actuate the two to provide the kind of reciprocal customer engagement that Gen C has demanded and Gen D will assume. This level of engagement is more vibrant precisely because you allow your newest customers to get exactly what they want out of a relationship with you—to participate, inform, and converse with you, while not being overtly sold to. This is the path to enabling Gen D's discovery.

A High-Definition Panorama

In a high-definition panorama, you move from black-and-white to color, and the increased detail, broader context, and greater amount of information brings new respect and new opportunities to earn customer trust.

Putting the customer into the kind of high definition you need to face the customerpocalypse is serious business. The challenge of achieving it could well be the tipping point for larger transformational changes in your organization, but the increased customer loyalty you will attain is more than sufficient reward. An even greater incentive is that if you fail to act, you run the risk of a steadily eroding customer base that puts your business on life support (at best).

As we have seen, this is not just about the all-around 360 of data. There needs to be a second and third 360 to incorporate intent and customer process. Add together the 360 data view, the 360 of intent, and the 360 of customer process, and you have hit 1080, which, perhaps ironically resonant with today's standards for television quality, is high definition. Sure, in TVs the specific 1080 resolution is being surpassed, but the metaphor still holds and the principle of high definition will always remain. If you've seen a hockey game on television and been able to follow the puck in a way you never were able to before high-def, you understand the principle. If you know how vain Hollywood stars are and how much they hate high-def because the camera shows their age and imperfections in ways makeup seems unable to hide, you understand the principle. Apply that understanding to your relationship with your customers, and the old 360 data customer view with which this discussion began, no matter how much data you may have, pales in comparison (pun intended).

DATA
Who

But to make this all work, you are going to have to stop paying lip service to "transforming technology" and fundamentally change how your entire enterprise thinks about, manages, and acquires technology. The stakes are too high. Kicking the technology can down the road is no longer an option, especially with today's competitive pressures and the looming presence of Gen D around the corner.

5

CHANGE HOW YOU THINK ABOUT TECHNOLOGY

Why is technology at the center of how you need to respond to the challenges described in the previous chapters? The answer is simple. Today, you have no chance of succeeding *without* information technology. It has already become a fundamental part of business, and for businesses that deal with diverse customer bases, have multiple products or services to sell, and do business in more than one location, the idea of going forward without technology is nothing short of ridiculous. Technology—and how it is used—is increasingly seen as the basis for differentiation and success in business.

Accenture Plc, a Fortune Global 500 company and one of the world's largest consulting firms (with which my own company has partnered commercially), gets it right in its Technology Vision 2013: "Without information and technology, a business is blind in today's digital world . . . Every business is now a digital business."[1]

The Accenture Vision continues: "The world has already changed around us, and IT is driving much of the transformation. IT is a minimum standard for how we effectively run our enterprise, but it has gone further than that. IT has become a driving force, in many situations *the* driving force, for how we effectively grow our companies. Every industry is now software driven; as such, every company must adopt IT as one of its core competencies. By this we mean that software is absolutely integral to how we currently run our businesses as well as how we reimagine our businesses as the world continues to change—how we redesign and produce things, how we create and manage new commercial transactions, how we begin to collaborate at unprecedented levels internally and with customers and suppliers. In the new world, our digital efforts will be the key to how we innovate and expand our business."

The Technology Vision is pointing to a Gen D world, particularly with respect to "collaborate . . . with customers . . ."

Finally, notes Accenture, "There is a higher order of thinking—a digital mind-set—that will, we believe, separate tomorrow's most able organizations from their lesser rivals."

One sign of the expanded, refined centrality of IT in business is that in many enterprises, the marketing function is eclipsing the information technology function as the main driver of technology spending, a trend that *Forbes* magazine reports "shows no sign or stopping—or even slowing down—any time soon."[2]

This is strong evidence that businesses have truly become digital businesses. For the longest time, information technology—which in the business world first served to automate accounting functions—mainly served internal operations. Now, IT has become fundamental to the outward-looking parts of the business, the customer-facing parts.

To accomplish a customer-centric approach, the *Forbes* article continues, "marketing needs systems in place for data collection, automated analysis and targeted distribution . . ." Marketing campaigns themselves are becoming "more and more centered on customer insight and real-time analytics."

Sound familiar?

Using digital technology is the single-most distinctive characteristic of the Gen D customers for whom you need to prepare. They use it to a degree that eclipses every generation that has come before them in business history, including Gen C.

As digitalization moves into the front office and the realm of your customers, it becomes absolutely critical that you make it succeed. The digital channel is now as fundamental as manufacturing once was. Manufacturing, once a key differentiator, became commoditized. The digital capabilities of a business are now a key differentiator. In fact, it is emerging as a core competency, central to how a business and its employees work, but also critical to achieving competitive advantage.

How critical? The correct "digital mind-set"—to use Accenture's phrase—is the difference between living and dying. Without information technology, there is no way you can break down the obstacles to the customer experience the ascendant Gen D demands. *No alternative exists.*

Your path to high-def, 1080 customer engagement that marries data, intent, and customer process into a powerful way to stay alive and thrive in the face of the coming Gen D, begins with changing how you think about technology. Everyone in your organization needs to change their mind-set, so that businesspeople and the information technology people alike, as well as the most senior executives, understand that technology should be first and foremost a way to optimize the customer experience and intelligently automate operations. Businesspeople need to understand that technology is what will ultimately get them where they need to go or cause them to fail, and they need to be able to believe that technology can be made available to them so they can genuinely serve their customers. The IT people need to relinquish a lot of control over decisions that were once thought to be the exclusive purview of the technologists. These are the *starting* preconditions to avoiding failure. We cannot, however, make it down this path with the awkward and unresponsive approach to business systems that characterizes how we have traditionally designed and delivered systems. We need more responsiveness, collaboration, and outside-in focus to be baked into our very approach to technology.

THE BUSINESS–IT COLLISION

Unfortunately, there is a lot to overcome before you can get there. Businesspeople are frustrated. They are hugely dissatisfied with information technology at their workplaces, because it does not do what they want. They wonder why their experiences at home, with great devices that easily do nearly anything they want, cannot be replicated at work. Why, they ask, has there been such an epic fail when it comes to achieving parity between the home and the office? They do not necessarily understand how dissimilar business systems are from their home devices, but even if they did, they probably would still insist on parity. After all, this is the twenty-first century! Going back even further, businesspeople want to know what happened to the promise of genuine business-oriented control of technology.

Consider just the people in your company's marketing function. "Marketers' confidence in today's technology management has flagged. They have doubts that it can offer the credibility, collaboration, and architecture to drive the business forward. Alarmingly, 32 percent of marketers believe that technology management actually hinders business success."[3]

"Hinders business success"! These factors are a large part of why the relationship between businesspeople and IT people in many companies is antithetical to one that helps the organization bring its customers into higher definition. There are too many issues of power and control and trust, and the history of the two sides routinely seeming to work at cross-purposes is too long.

Businesspeople do not necessarily know what they need to know about the IT side and what it takes to build a new system but often think they do. At the same time, IT people are too often wedded to their archaic ways of doing things, expressed in the form of a traditional development process that has largely gone unchanged over the past four decades. On top of that, IT faces enormous pressures on their budgets and views business demands as more than can be afforded.

A host of other issues get in the way of IT's effectiveness. Mergers and acquisitions distract them from anything but figuring out how to glue disparate systems together. In most enterprises, they are minding a large legacy system environment and spend about 80 percent of their time and money trying to maintain existing systems, rather than thinking about where the business is going and how they might help. Faced with all these pressures, they lapse back into old approaches or try to find some miraculous and unconventional solution. All this exacerbates the already broken relationship with businesspeople and compels businesspeople to look for alternatives that end up weakening the overall effort.

How computers are programmed and how decisions are made about which systems to build, are at the root of the disconnect between business and IT, two vitally important parts of your enterprise. Let's look at how each of them got to where we are today.

HOW COMPUTER PROGRAMMING BECAME A MESS

When computers first began to be used in business, systems were built on programming that was all 0s and 1s. This binary notation represented the instructions for the machine to perform its elementary operations. It was a language for computers, machine language or machine *code*, by which programmers told the computer's central processing unit to execute this or that task. Numerical machine code of this sort is about as stripped down a language for computers as there is.

This underlying need for translation has remained a constant, for the most part. As new languages came along, with translation still governing the relationship between businesspeople and the machine, the need for specialized skills to program a machine to approximate what businesspeople needed the machine to do grew stronger. The gulf between business and IT widened as the expectations of what computers could and should do increased and expanded.

Numerical machine code gave way to assembly code, which eliminated a lot of the tedium of the earlier language, and reduced some of the errors but did not introduce an actual business language to computer programming. Assembly languages still were intended to be translators, taking a series of low-level processor instructions and meta-statements, comments, and data, and translating them into machine language instructions that could be put in a computer's memory and executed.

Things did improve, but only with respect to the languages of the machine themselves, not in bridging that gap between business and IT. Fortran (derived from Formula Translating System) came along in the 1950s, moving programming closer to things that make sense to people by using a more symbolic language. But it was truly a technical language for engineers.

Then COBOL arrived, aimed primarily for use in business, finance, and administrative systems and professing to get programming closer to the language of business. COBOL is an acronym for Common Business-Oriented Language—but putting the word "business" into the language's name did not change things. Businesspeople didn't use COBOL; IT people remained the programmers, and COBOL was still a translation tool far distant from what businesspeople would understand.

BASIC arrived, emphasizing ease of use for less-technical programmers. The acronym stands for Beginner's All-Purpose Symbolic

Instruction Code, and the general purpose language did make it possible for some small business owners to create their own small applications on personal computers. But even Business BASIC didn't change that you still had to be a *programmer* to create a system. I had the privilege of learning BASIC at college from its creators John Kemeny and Thomas Kurtz—but no one ever pretended it was really business-oriented. The language was always viewed from the computational steps, the data structures, the mechanics, and the machine's perspective of the technical implementation.

Along the historical path of computer languages, we eventually got to object-oriented languages. These represent an attempt to abstract a higher order of logic patterns and prevent the ugly "spaghetti code" that was so easy to implement in other programming paradigms. In object-oriented programming, "objects" are concepts with properties that describe them (think data fields). Associated procedures are called "methods." Design of applications happens by using the objects to interact with each other. But these changes actually made understanding what was going on even more complicated and more abstract.

Then so-called fourth-generation programming languages (4GLs) were born . . . and died. Their intent was to supersede the third-generation languages (3GLs) based more on higher level concepts and often tied to database specific implementations by technologists who believed that applications could be developed more rapidly if some kind of language and method could just generate the equivalent of 3GLs' instructions but with fewer errors. Overall, the target was reductions in time, effort, and cost to develop systems. But they were misguided in targeting the wrong end of the challenge—they were tools for engineers rather than capabilities that would allow the businesspeople to become involved in getting the technology to do what they wanted.

In the history of programming languages, new ones are introduced time and again that are supposed to make it easier for people to program. However, it seems clear that after COBOL and the stated goal of getting closer to business, languages actually moved in the opposite direction, away from business. After all, how likely is it that a *business* programming language would employ the same mental model as in traditional programming?

Java—today's predominant programming language—is a great example of this move backward, of a retreat to the orientation of the machine. Its origins can be traced to 1991 under different names. By 1995, Sun Microsystems was releasing its first public implementation, known as Java 1.0. Sun's promise was "write once, run anywhere" (WORA), and because of this it became very popular. WORA means code that runs on one platform does not need to be recompiled to run on another. It was specifically designed to be general purpose and to have as few implementation dependencies as possible. Pretty soon, it was ubiquitous, with new versions that had multiple configurations built for different types of platforms. Eventually, among young computer geeks, it became *sine qua non* to know Java.

Today, there are millions of Java programmers around the world working for themselves and for companies large and small. Sure, Java is better than many other computer languages in many respects, but the paradigm for Java is still the old one that has kept business and IT people separated, ever since the advent of computing—dedicated programmers are required and the way the technology is instructed to operate bears no resemblance to how businesspeople would describe what they do. For businesspeople, this means they must still go to translators to get their technology needs met. In reality, from a business point of view, ancient COBOL is actually more intelligible than Java—though still divorced from the way businesspeople think.

The way computers are programmed, though, is only one of two big disconnects between what business needs and how technology tries to serve those needs. The other disconnect is in how systems development projects are prioritized.

TRADITIONAL DEVELOPMENT

The lack of understanding about technology on the business side of the enterprise can be illustrated with an analogy. Think of the IT professional as the architect and the businessperson as the client who hires the architect to build an addition to her house. The client has a pretty good idea of what she wants. She's been to Home Depot and she reads *House Beautiful* magazine. When it comes to room additions, she's come to understand what is off the shelf, standard, and customized. She knows about bay windows and French doors, and her trips to Home Depot have taught her that doorframes are a standard width and that anything else requires extra work and extra money. She also knows there's a standard size for ceiling tiles, which means lots and lots of choices, and that anything other than the standard size will not only increase her costs in the beginning, but make it impossible to take advantage of off-the-shelf options should she choose to change the ceiling tiles sometime in the future.

So, the client and the architect can have an informed and very pragmatic discussion. She has a lot to tell him. They discuss not only what the room is for, and how the client wants the room to look, but she is able to stipulate a lot of specific design characteristics. Of course, the architect has opinions, and is certainly capable of introducing alternative ideas, even radical ones. But they talk at a very concrete level about windows and doors and the ceiling and the paint color, and so on. The client has been empowered to have that concrete discussion.

Let's contrast this to the typical interaction between business and IT. In the current development model, most of what businesspeople tell IT people is defined abstractly. IT people tell businesspeople not to worry about implementation. With this type of vague interaction at a system's inception, is it really any wonder that confusion, miscommunication, and needlessly expensive choices slip in?

Here is how the traditional development process works in today's typical company. Businesspeople have an idea for how to make things more efficient with customers, or better serve some customer segment, or deal with a new regulation that affects customers. To implement the idea, some kind of new business service based on a software solution is necessary. Businesspeople will have to work with IT.

The process begins with businesspeople writing a requirements document that is supposed to tell IT what the solution must do. The objective is to get *everything* into that document that might matter over the next three to four years, because it is the only chance—since it is unlikely there will ever be a version 2 of the system in any predictable timeframe. So, the requirements document becomes an epic act of imagination, a statement of 150 percent of what any business could ever possibly need to cover anticipated and imagined objectives.

There is also no useful feedback loop; once the IT people get the requirements document, the back-and-forth commences through awkward and abstract discussions that rarely highlight the cost (or time) difference for alternatives in a way that fosters rational business decision-making. Eventually, through multiple iterations, the document expresses something everyone believes can actually be developed. So, the IT folks turn around and create design specs.

You'd be hard pressed to find a business or IT person at a company who will tell you that the design specs truly reflect the requirements document, or vice versa. Yet, the specs get turned into code, typically over an extended period of a year or a year and a half. The traditional development process is nothing if not slow. By the time users test the application, it corresponds to a customer-related idea that is old itself, and that is a big problem as Gen D barrels down on your business. And, the code is at least four generations removed from the original idea—they have gone through "functional decomposition," "technical decomposition," and "data decomposition," and are then typed into text files as cryptic words to be compiled into the language of the machine. By the time all this decomposition has been done, you really do have the makings of a computer system version of the walking dead. These zombie systems, whether built on top of some purchased and then customized software or built from scratch, are intrinsically unresponsive and stagnant. Once the programs are actually written, they bear little or no resemblance to the original specifications. This is because the traditional development process imposes such an enormous gap between how a system is specified, how it is manually programmed, and then again how it is documented. All of this creates a shaky foundation for making any changes, because the gap between need and implementation, coupled with poor documentation, makes change frightening.

This specification gap plays out commonly in steps. There is a weak blueprint from the outset, so the system developers make poor architectural decisions. Repeated changes in specifications make the blueprint even weaker. As requirements are added to the system and it falls further and further behind schedule, scope creep ensues and the code gets bloated with little reuse. Often, the final *coup de grâce* is the plan to launch the system with a big bang, switching users virtually overnight, which makes it nearly impossible to adopt any parts of the system until the whole is "perfect."

Traditional development is sometimes called the "waterfall model." Businesspeople and IT people go through requirements, design, implementation, verification, and end up in maintenance, step-by-step, flowing like water heading down the river—and over the cliff.

Source: DILBERT © 1999 Scott Adams. Used By permission of UNIVERSAL UCLICK. All rights reserved.

To be sure, the waterfall analogy isn't perfect, but it does highlight many of the issues for concern. Real waterfalls are beautiful. They draw us to them as tourists and delight us when we see them. But the waterfalls of the traditional development process are artificial and rarely make anyone smile, because it is a highly dysfunctional way to get things done. For example, the serial nature highlights the lack of feedback, and the eventual deliverable comes crashing, like Niagara Falls, to earth, often with terrifying force and results.

Inevitably, businesspeople are going to need changes that will make the system reflect how they really do business, either because things have changed, or something's missing, or both. But those changes cost money and time.

All told, the traditional development process creates three fundamental technology problems—zombie systems, manual systems, and rogue systems—all of which have at their root the simple fact that businesspeople are not getting what they need.

Zombie Systems

Zombie systems are systems that stagnate when businesspeople need changes to optimize the customer experience, but can never get those changes implemented. Zombie systems are an epidemic in the business world.

One of the main villains behind stagnant zombie systems is the IT portfolio management process used to allocate scarce capital. It has evolved in concert with (and to help control) the waterfall model. It is analogous to managing an investment portfolio, and there is a good chance your company uses it. The basic idea sounds seductively rational: Determine which projects to invest in by understanding exactly what you are going to spend on each potential project and what the return on investment (ROI) will be.

Of course, the portfolio management process does not solve the long-standing debate on how best to measure the value of an IT investment. Nevertheless, it forces the business side to propose a portfolio of what it wants and needs. From that list, scarce resources are allocated among various parts of the business side (channels, silos, and so on). In essence, competition is created around a culture of scarcity and famine.

The combination of the waterfall and the portfolio management process leads to tight control over software availability. You create a dam to manage the flow of resources, much like creating a reservoir. In that reservoir are all the desires for the technology businesspeople need, analogous to the water held back by the dam. In nature, the water flows continuously over the waterfall, but in the portfolio management process, the water is released selectively, in the form of development projects. The people who control the reservoir have to be convinced to open the sluice gates. Out from the sluice gates of the artificial dam comes whatever project is released, and the water pounds down into the business over the artificially created waterfall. You better have made the right decision before you open those sluice gates, yet that is hard to do given the vagaries of defining what will be in a project, let alone dealing with the reality of what actually gets delivered from the typical technology project.

The portfolio management process is intended to ensure that the most important IT investments are made, but it is enormously frustrating to businesspeople. And it sets up a self-fulfilling prophecy. The portfolio management process, in the context of the traditional development process, drives this culture of overspecification. The entire paradigm is geared to large, overdesigned projects that have overestimated ROIs. You propose a big, important-looking system so it will rise to the top. The projects that make it to the top of the list eat up all the available resources, so there is never a chance for a version 2 (on that or other projects) where you could make important incremental changes that ultimately can continuously improve customer experience and business efficiency. Without the chance for ongoing change, everything stagnates. Knowing that projects always stagnate, businesspeople overspecify next time, too, just to try and get as much into the next development cycle as possible. It is a self-perpetuating, dysfunctional reality of system development in enterprises.

Manual Systems

Next, we come to manual systems, which are efforts to work around stagnant zombie (or even missing) systems. Of course, a common reaction to a stagnant system is to try fixing it by adding a manual system. Take credit card disputes. Credit card issuers know that the business rules for disputes can become set in stone and become impossible to change in the system, so they end up deciding to deal with key aspects of disputes manually. Who can blame them? When businesspeople don't get what they need through the traditional development process, they find workarounds. Sometimes, because the expectations of what systems will deliver are so low, businesspeople will even specify approaches that turn tasks over to people, even though they could be done by the system, just to maintain some ability to change processes without having to reenter the portfolio management process and beg for something new.

Not all manual systems eschew the technology route completely. Some are built around Excel spreadsheets or simple databases, but all have the characteristic of being low-automation. Others are completely manual, implemented through the creation of policies and training rather than using an effective level of automation. Some are combinations of both.

For example, a bank may end up with a zombie lending system that makes it possible to book loans and do accruals, but provides no guidance to users on the correct credit limit to establish for a given customer, or what the risk consequences to the bank might be of a certain lending decision. So, business users create a manual system as a workaround. But the manual system lacks the ability to ensure reliable execution of critical processes, and people are largely trusted to remember and execute all the right procedures and calculations. This leads to the kind of disaster we have seen in the past and that is surely destined to repeat—all because the users perceive they lack good alternatives.

Thus the issue of zombie systems actually creates an impetus for the introduction of manual systems. Because users are afraid their systems will stagnate, some major systems are designed for extensive human intervention as the only way to address the fact that needed incremental changes in existing systems are never going to happen in time.

Manual systems can be a colossal waste of time, using up human resources that could be so much more effectively employed if people had the right technological tools with which to do their jobs. One example is the "fingernet," which involves toggling between multiple screens on a computer to do work that could be in one screen, if the system had been built correctly, or where a person works on one screen and then swivels his chair around to type some information into another computer device. Human fingers replacing the ability of the computer to do simple standardized tasks—truly a reversal of what we would expect from the power of technology.

Another problem is that manual procedures typically leave out lots of the things that ought to be in a real system, like safeguards and controls. The results can be devastating. It was the combination of zombie systems and manual systems that brought down the venerable Barings

Bank in 1995. Trader Nick Leeson was able to game the system, circumventing the bank's internal auditing and risk-management controls and ultimately running up losses of $1.4 billion in about a month-and-a-half.

What happened in April and May 2012 at JPMorgan is another story of that same combination of stagnant and manual resulting in disaster by limiting visibility into what is really going on. Transactions booked through the firm's London branch led to massive trading losses. A highly secretive trader named Bruno Iksil, nicknamed "the London Whale," accumulated outsized positions on derivatives known as credit default swaps, and some $6.2 billion was lost.[4] Criminal investigations into the firm's risk-management system and internal controls followed, and JPMorgan was fined $920 million.[5]

Fortunately, not all manual systems have these kinds of impacts. Unfortunately, businesses have yet to learn the important lesson they teach: They foster a lack of transparency; they are subject to inconsistent application of policies and rules; they can make businesses the victims of innocent mistakes or intentional gaming; and they can lead to enormous fines and even the death of a business enterprise.

ROGUE SYSTEMS

Finally, there are the rogue systems. These are the result of businesspeople, frustrated beyond words, creating well-intentioned but poorly conceived stopgaps to address their needs. They want automation to build processes and rules into their systems. They would prefer to go the mainstream route, but they get caught in the stagnant swamp of the portfolio management process. So they end up, unintentionally, making it difficult to do business well.

Business users who are so desperate and frustrated can end up building huge portfolios of makeshift applications and systems that are completely unsustainable. Make your way through the vast landscape of the business world, and the number of systems you'll see built entirely on complex macros in an Excel spreadsheet will be staggering. The idea that this is the way to optimize the customer experience or intelligently automate operations is laughable, if it weren't so potentially devastating.

Citibank's Global Transaction Services (GTS) division faced this rogue systems problem. GTS provides Citi clients in more than 100 countries with a variety of integrated treasury and trade solutions, along with securities and fund services. These highly demanding clients are multinational corporations, other financial institutions, and public sector institutions. GTS is supposed to serve local and cross-border interests alike. Today, the service is considered world-class, well-coordinated, and a powerful competitive differentiator. But it wasn't always so.

At one time, Citi GTS operated without global consistency. There were dozens of baby systems across the globe to track and manage customer service. These systems had grown up over years, as businesspeople—absent being able to get the IT support they wanted and needed or quite happy to do things their own way—built dozens of them to track service interactions and serve their customers. Some were the result of regional development efforts. Others emerged from skunkworks. Sometimes, they were manual systems using tools such as Excel to maintain this or that list.

Imagine what happened when a huge multinational like PepsiCo came to Citi GTS for services, expecting seamlessness and integration. The Citi account manager had no way to get a unified, global picture of PepsiCo as a customer. The information was dissipated across many islands of automation. Meanwhile, PepsiCo might get a different answer to the same question asked in Detroit and Dubai.

Fortunately, Citi GTS today has all countries on one service backbone, providing overall control to ensure best-in-class service to customers, but with enough flexibility so local offices can do what they need to do that differs from place to place. It was the result of a thoughtful campaign that brought together the right technology and values to convince senior management and the individual units how much better life would be for them and their clients with a coherent approach.

SHADOW IT

The discipline and teamwork at Citi that brought the groups into alignment is in stark contrast to most companies that have faced the rogue systems problem. In some firms, the creation of and attempts to maintain rogue systems has even become institutionalized, with businesspeople increasingly developing their own systems and solutions without organizational approval, often taking on technology challenges that are well beyond their capacity and leading to disastrous results.

"Business divisions are bypassing the IT department, making their own decisions to buy cloud-based application services or use mobile devices, raising the specter of so-called 'shadow IT' that's outside the knowledge or control of the CIO and the IT staff."[6]

It is unsustainable, and it puts tremendous *bad* pressure on the already strained relationship between the business and technology sides of the enterprise. "Now Shadow IT has burst out of the closet and is waltzing around the corporation, leaving IT departments rushing to do damage control."[7]

These Shadow IT systems sometimes lack even have the basic password controls and other things you'd implement in a serious corporate system. Yet, they are used to manage critical aspects of the business—that is, until they break, the "rogues" are caught, or they end up with some massive failure revealed on the front pages of the *Wall Street Journal* or *Financial Times*.

MIND THE GAP?

There are lots of people out there who think they have the answer to how the gap between the great experiences at home and the crappy experiences at work can be bridged. Of the many possible examples, let's just look at one. The Object Management Group (OMG),[8] an international industry consortium founded in 1989, is a not-for-profit group with membership open to any organization, large or small. OMG's mission statement includes "to develop . . . integration standards that provide real-world value" and the group's members "share experiences in transitioning to new management and technology approaches like Cloud Computing."

OMG is a good example because of its wide scope. Over the years, OMG task forces have worked on a broad range of technologies and modeling standards, all of which have been touted by various analysts as "next-big-thing" approaches that could solve many of the problems you've read about in the earlier chapters. They run the gamut from "Architecture-Driven Modernization" to "Model-Driven Architecture," from "Real-time, Embedded and Specialized Systems" to the "Unified Modeling Language."

Model-Driven Architecture (MDA) is a big deal to OMG people. It is a software design approach launched by OMG in 2001 that provides a set of guidelines for how to structure specifications, which in MDA are expressed as models. It is supposed to make system design more effective by enabling abstract modeling from which an automated tool can derive some or all of the source code necessary for the software system.

However, as is pretty typical with gaps, how you think it ought to be addressed can be influenced heavily by which side of the gap you happen to be standing on. OMG stands firmly on the tech side. Thus, the OMG committee that governs MDA conceives of it as a way to define technology, not business. And with its roots in the technical domain, the types of models that can be designed are aimed at technologists. So, whatever promise it may have, it remains trapped in the old paradigm of technology first. You can be "model driven" yet still rely on arcane technical metaphors that are miles from how businesspeople think of what they are trying to accomplish for customers. The outside-in world, starting from the customer's vantage point, operates in an entirely different universe.

THE DESPERATION BANDWAGON

Out of desperation, businesses are looking for magic bullets and quick fixes to solve their systems problems. One seat on the desperation bandwagon is offshore development. Sending work offshore does not solve the fundamental problems that have led to all the bad outcomes described earlier. It just moves the problems somewhere else. The only real difference in how your system gets built is that it's being done by people half a world away, most likely in India. Those programmers, though, are still building your system the old-fashioned way, using the traditional development process.

Actually, having huge pools of less-expensive but distant software coders only makes things worse. When the systems development work is sent offshore, you are exacerbating the dysfunction of an already dysfunctional process. Perhaps even making the dysfunction come to the fore faster!

Another seat on the desperation bandwagon is cloud computing, the use of hardware and software resources as a service that is delivered over the Internet. It is becoming ubiquitous. You cannot watch television for any extended period without seeing some advertisement touting this or that technology "leveraging the power of the cloud." But as is often the case in the hype cycle, this gets teed up to address way more challenges than it effectively can.

There is no question that the cloud continues to enable accelerated deployments of systems by eliminating delays due to infrastructure and providing an elasticity to address unanticipated changes in demand. It offers a way to reduce friction around deployment and capital expenditures. But in terms of changing the way your systems are *built*, the cloud offers nothing. And something those ads don't mention is that when you use the cloud, you are entrusting your data, software, and computation to some remote service. In short, the cloud may be fine for certain uses, but there are serious pitfalls if your goal is to create a system that is agile not just in infrastructure but also in business content.

Still, the cloud is a big part of Gen D's online world. So, a lot of those who sell business technology like to present cloud computing as doing what the cool kids are doing. That is why so much new development at companies today is focused on iPads and Facebook and Twitter. And that is why a growing number of your employees are probably bringing their own devices and software to work. You have probably seen this trend unfold, especially with younger employees, as they try to bridge the gap by using their own tools, the ones with which they've long been satisfied.

Could the cloud and commoditized software offered as a service possibly substitute for customer processes like those described in Chapter 4? Would you put your memory and judgment and muscle into someone else's *generic* body, and assume that it will magically function in a way that serves your interests best? Of course not. The thought that what is basically a deployment choice will intrinsically best serve your customers' intent in a personalized, differentiated, and responsive fashion is ludicrous.

At a more technical level, you face immense challenges integrating cloud services with your existing systems. Trying to achieve the heavy degree of customization you'd need to approach genuine customer processes can be considerably more expensive than anything your IT people might build from scratch. So, while the cloud may address some infrastructure and support problems, it does not even *begin* to help you answer these questions: What does the cloud do to help make me special to my customers? And if I create separate systems in the cloud, how will I achieve the needed high-def integration of data, intent, and process?

Indeed, the cloud is now the breeding ground for the next generation of rogue systems—hacked together and suffering from poor maintainability and stagnation. Fortune 500 computer security software company Symantec conducted a global survey and reported in early 2013 that a huge majority of businesses are seeing costs rise from "rogue cloud implementations."[9] These rogue cloud implementations take the form of businesspeople implementing public cloud applications that no one on the IT side of the enterprise manages, integrates into the company's IT infrastructure, or—in many cases—*even knows about!*

Beyond the costs, the security issues are monumental.

"So why are organizations doing it?" the report asks. "One in five don't realize they shouldn't. However, the most commonly cited reason for these rogue cloud projects was to save time and money: Going through IT would make the process more difficult."

So, before you even have a chance to fight off Gen D's efforts to kill your business, your own people might help your business commit suicide.

AGILE PROGRAMMING TO THE RESCUE?

Some alternatives have been put forward to solve the problems of the traditional development process and the zombie, manual, and rogue systems to which it leads. One of them is agile software development.

It is helpful, to a degree, but it is also inadequate for addressing the core issue of getting technology to be as responsive as it must become.

First introduced in the 2001 "Manifesto for Agile Software Development,"[10] it is based on an iterative and incremental development model in which requirements and solutions are meant to evolve. The process is collaborative, meant to involve crossfunctional teams that organize themselves to get the work done. As such, it is quite different from the relationship described earlier between business and IT people, and much closer to that of the architect and client. It goes in the right direction.

However, agile development does not solve the fundamental problems. Too often, agile development projects are still subject to the portfolio management process, which means the selection process will still preclude version 2 and beyond. Thus it often continues to subject business users to an overly burdensome specifications activity that ultimately leads to the same old inflexible and nonevolving systems you get from traditional development. In other words, "agile" in a waterfall culture becomes zombie. You just get to zombie systems faster. What you really need is agile development in an agile *culture*.

This is why even in organizations that have adopted agile programming to a significant degree, businesspeople still create a lot of manual systems and the rogue systems pop up all over.

READY TO CHANGE?

Organizational managers have known for years that there are far too many holes in the ways they control processes and the judgment and risk built into those processes. Unfortunately, they have had little choice but to go along with manual processes or semiautomated, disjointed rogue systems simply because to do otherwise would likely grind business to a halt. When businesspeople undertake projects that end up as manual and rogue systems, they institutionalize gaps in the processes and controls across *entire* companies. Yes, they are just trying to find a way to get their work done, but they do not necessarily create systems that incorporate sound business judgment. The consequences can be far greater than missing some new business opportunity. In fact, as the Barings Bank and JPMorgan examples illustrate, they can be devastating.

It's not hard to fathom why these systems emerge, especially when you consider that businesspeople and IT people have been working at what seems to be cross-purposes for so long, and that often they seem incapable of communicating effectively. Meanwhile, the IT team struggles to support and maintain all this stuff, they get angry at businesspeople who appear continually dissatisfied, and the cycle of fighting over control goes on and on.

So, what do you do? MDA, the cloud, just about every so-called solution described earlier is a placebo. And while the sentiment to replicate at work the positive experiences people have with their home devices is a worthy one, home technology is not the path to genuine business technology. The reason is simple: The design for home technology, all those things that begin with "i," is geared to the individual. That is completely reasonable, but it cannot substitute for business technology. In a business setting, technology should no more be organized around the IT people than it should be organized around the *individual* businessperson. It has to be organized around the customer, enabling agility, data, intent, and customer processes.

As laid out at the beginning of this chapter, your starting point for optimizing the customer experience, intelligently automating operations, and bringing your customers into high-definition is to change how everyone in your organization thinks about technology. It is the precursor to changing how you create and use systems. Clearly, the traditional development approach that led you into zombie, manual, and rogue systems has to go. You have to ditch those requirements and design specs that are part of the waterfall model. You need a rational approach to the totality of your technology, driven by business decisions and not by the individual and highly controlled "sluice gate" mentality. You have to change the collaboration model between your business and IT people, so that systems are being built based on the language of business, defined by the people who will use them and who will interact with your customers. Ultimately, everything must be about the customer.

The technology you need to embrace is something that can make it possible to combine the data 360, intent 360, and customer processes 360. If you don't understand that, you will never achieve them all working together as 1080.

And yet, even with all that, you cannot rely only on changing things about the technology. Technology is more important than ever before because of the digital environment that breeds Gen D expectations and assumptions, but it is not the only imperative when it comes to preparing for the customerpocalypse. You need to change your organization, too, liberating it from the shackles of old thinking and old models. Let's look at how.

6

LIBERATING YOUR
ORGANIZATION

Source: Delacroix, Eugene (1798–1863). July 28th, 1830. Liberty guiding the people, detail. Musée de Louvre, Paris, France. Photo credit: Erich Lessing/Art Resource, NY. Used with permission.

Whe n a leading U.S. company in the benefits management business began to bring its customers into 1080 high-definition, the senior leadership quickly realized that it needed to completely rethink how it organized, hired, trained, and rewarded its people as part of an entirely new way of doing business. The company established a radically new organizational structure better suited to close collaboration with its connected customer base and one that would enhance the customer experience. Its model is a good one for other businesses to adopt.

Just as with changing the relationship between business and IT, an organization that wants to enter this 1080 high-def world has no choice but to change the structure of how it harnesses technology. But it's not enough simply to adopt what you think of as a new strategy and shift things around on the organizational chart. There also has to be a culture change. As the remark famously attributed to management consultant and author Peter Drucker goes: "Culture eats strategy for breakfast."

How do you get there? One step involves fundamentally changing the relationship between business and IT in your organization. It stands to reason that if you are going to undertake the kind of transformation discussed in Chapter 5 with respect to how technology is thought of, developed, and used, that relationship is going to have to undergo some serious changes.

Hybrid Vigor for Business and IT

Lots of enterprises make organizational changes that affect how business and IT people interact, sometimes even aligning their reporting within the company. But to transform that relationship in the context of becoming Gen D friendly, a customer-centric, high-def organization, you have to go even further and align the two in new ways. One approach to achieving that objective is to cross-pollinate, just like in the plant world. Cross-pollination occurs when pollen is delivered to a flower from a different plant. Most plants have adapted to reproducing through cross-pollination, and the plant world has developed a host of mechanisms to maximize this virtuous circle of fertilization and reproduction.

What makes cross-pollination a good thing? The answer is simple: You combine the best pieces of DNA from multiple sources to create a strong, new whole.

Enterprises can benefit from the same concept, and cross-pollination's praises have been sung in the business world for some time. "Cross-pollination is big these days. Whether you are a retailer or a research lab, the gospel is that if you mix things up you'll get a creative ferment," wrote Lee Fleming in a decade-old *Harvard Business Review* article.[1]

I suggest going even further. Consider one of the benefits of cross-pollination that leads to something truly transformative—*heterosis* or *hybrid vigor*, the improved or increased vigor or other superior qualities that arise when genetically different plants or animals are crossbred. Heterosis is the term used to describe this phenomenon when the parents are taken from different populations of the same species, while hybrid vigor is used when the parents come from different species. You may argue that businesspeople and IT people are just different populations of the same species, but decades of observation suggest that hybrid vigor is the appropriate term here.

For instance, the benefits management company mentioned at the beginning of this chapter undertook a major cross-pollination effort that included a massive revamp of its organizational structure. Hundreds of employees were pulled out of the IT organization to help populate a new world. They were sent to work directly with the business lines as part of "innovation centers." Management created a healthy and competitive innovation incubator that rewarded the right kind of investments in projects to enhance the customer experience. Funding and incentives were tied to these projects' success in generating real business results within a short period, typically a financial quarter.

The innovation centers were supported, in turn, by business process centers that ensured consistent and excellent processes across all channels. Of course, IT continued to support the horizontal plumbing needed by the innovation teams to get their jobs done, but without distracting them from their critical customer-facing processes.

This all resulted in a form of hybrid vigor. In the new environment, behaviors and expectations changed. Business and IT people working together in the innovation centers began to pull together in ways they had never done before. They saw themselves as part of a team, not as users and providers of a service. The cross-pollination began work to change the mind-set and culture of the business and IT people, which was then reinforced by the organizational change.

Over time, the business and IT people in the innovation centers underwent a radical shift together. They became like the architect and homeowner client of Chapter 5. The architect brought technical knowledge to the discussion, and the client was fully empowered to have a concrete discussion about the technology.

It's like a matrix, but it goes even further. Common processes were defined across business lines. Then, whatever could be standardized and synthesized was done consistently, while individual lines of business were still allowed to set out on their own in situations where that was necessary. By serving customers uniformly, with intent and process guiding each interaction, the customer experience is always in high-def. The shared framework for common business processes made the business agile and adaptable, and the management structure reflected these characteristics. The IT staff maintained an architecture that is manageable, predictable, and logical. And the management structure reinforced this, too.

The chief operating officer at the time said that the organizational shift to innovation centers dramatically reduced operating expenses, thanks to the redesign of the core processes. He also described all the cash it generated over time. The projected 30-percent productivity gain over 10 years created a tremendously high return on invested capital.

Another example, ING Poland, has realized tremendous benefits, too. As part of a strategic initiative to modernize its sales and distribution capabilities, the company set out to standardize and merge individual processes in a way that brought together best practices. Thanks to the effort, the captive agent sales force (those selling only ING products) was completely modernized. Agents could be up and running, selling to customers, within eight weeks, when it had taken six months before the initiative. ING Poland extended its market leadership by expanding into new sales areas with new products and opening up new distribution channels, all of which took advantage of commonalities in processes. The achievement of 80 percent reuse of processes was a phenomenal statistic.

Of course, cross-pollination and hybrid vigor for a company requires a vehicle for manifesting DNA, for capturing all of a company's digital DNA—the company's unique "you-ness"—and making it part of every customer engagement in a way that makes the customer *want to engage*. That happens through your software, which is the technological manifestation of your customer processes and your outside-in way of engaging with customers.

BREAK THE GRIPS OF CHANNELS AND SILOS

No two organizations need to follow exactly the same path to cross-pollination. There are a few guiding principles to follow, and then you can construct the solution that makes the most sense for your particular circumstance. Look at the opportunities in your enterprise. What is common but isn't organized with commonality in mind? What can be made common? Build on that. Find everything that can be done in common across channels, silos, departments, and so on. It's the beginning of thinking in layers. You do this by identifying everything from the customer perspective. And you look for things that seem to have, or sound like they have, similar attributes. Inevitably, they've been cobbled together in individual silos.

This can be more difficult than it may seem. Typically, when enterprises try to plan for reuse and shared processes, the entrenched organizations within the enterprise insist that everything they do is unique and has little or nothing in common with other departments or lines of business. That is rarely the case.

"We had a group of people on the clinical side come together a little while ago, and they all thought that they did a certain piece of work very differently, says a senior IT leader at a top-five U.S. health care organization. "When you peeled . . . the onion . . . they were all doing pretty much the same thing, but there was this 5 percent of difference in the processes."[2]

Those differences, she continued, "were more around the regional or localities that they were operating in . . . If you understand that those are the things that are different, those are the things you can start to build into your model."

With that understanding, you can make it possible for every channel, silo, and department to snap into core processes and vice versa. This is the third of the 360s that make up 1080 customer high-def. If a channel has an order processing issue, there should be only one place to go to get it addressed, and it needs to be addressed in a way that crosses every product line in the organizational structure.

REALIGN EXECUTIVE LEADERSHIP

Some organizations have gone even further, establishing a new executive position called chief process officer (CPO). This is recognition of just how important it is to elevate the visibility of and attention to critical customer processes throughout the enterprise. In large part, it is geared to the idea that as the business goes to market in whatever vertical setting, the correct horizontal leverage points have been uncovered and are being put to effective use.

At *Telstra,* Australia's leading telecommunications and information services company, there has been a recognition by senior leadership that process excellence is a critical driver of the firm's number-one strategic priority—improving customer service. Telstra's vision for process excellence has meant making changes to the company's operating model and introducing enabling technology. Central to this all has been dedicated executive coordination. That is why the company, which builds and operates telecommunications networks and markets voice, mobile, Internet access, and pay television products and services to millions of Australian customers, has an executive and general manager leading a team *specifically* for process excellence.

Peter McDonald, General Manager Process Excellence, explains what it means to "lead in the marketplace" and points to why having genuine executive leadership is so important. Telstra, he says, must "really understand what customers want and then [be] able to translate that into specific designable requirements and then improve our processes, deliver . . . not just their needs, but their wants, but also then their 'wows.'"

Telstra gets the difference between the old way of looking at processes and the idea of *customer processes* as discussed in Chapter 4. "All good processes must start with the customer," McDonald says.[3] "Good process is invisible to customers, but that's really the key to driving your business because the customer is not really interested in [all the other things you do] except making a transformation of inputs through process to outcomes. That's process management . . ." as Telstra sees it.

"Your business," McDonald emphasizes, "is your process." The customer process excellence for which McDonald is responsible includes a new order activation system that gives Telstra employees real-time visibility from start to finish, allows them to identify choke points, and features continuous improvement across the enterprise. Time-consuming tasks have been simplified or eliminated; teams have been consolidated to reduce handoffs; roles and responsibilities across the service chain have been clarified; and key performance indicators have been defined. In one product line, Telstra is seeing a reduced cycle time for order-to-activation by 70 percent, and customer satisfaction is on the rise.

The wows have resulted from the very tailoring of processes for customers described in Chapter 4.

There is also a chief customer officer (CCO) role emerging as part of realigning executive leadership. Forrester analysts Harley Manning and Paul Hagen, for example, have taken note of the growing number of enterprises that have made an organizational commitment to putting the customer into high-definition by establishing this position. In his book with Kerry Bodine, Manning explains how CCOs may range from playing a purely advisory role, to a matrixed role across functional roles, to being given full operational authority.[4]

Most CCOs, it turns out, are former division presidents or general managers or come from the marketing, sales, or operations organizations. That some are maturing into roles with wide, direct operational oversight is a sign of the times.

REDESIGN THE ROLE OF CUSTOMER SERVICE

You will also need to determine just how you are going to match customer intentions with business intent and based on that, define new roles for customer service. This is a major undertaking. The model of customer service that will correspond to what Gen D demands bears little resemblance to how the overwhelming majority of businesses do customer service now. But the fact is that no enterprise can move its customers to 1080 high-definition if it is stuck in the past. The change begins with throwing out the old way of thinking.

Consider some of the traditional explanations of what customer service means. Think about these in the context of what you now know about enhancing the customer experience to bring customers into high-definition, and what it might mean for people in your enterprise who interact with customers.

Customer service, says BusinessDictionary.com, is "All interactions between a customer and product provider at the time of sale, and thereafter. Customer service adds value to product and builds enduring relationships."[5] Investopedia puts it this way: "The process of ensuring customer satisfaction with a product or service. Often, customer service takes place while performing a transaction for the customer, such as making a sale or returning an item. Customer service can take the form of an in-person interaction, a phone call, self-service systems, or by other means."[6]

Wikipedia's article on the topic turns to a textbook for its definition. "Customer service is a series of activities designed to enhance the level of customer satisfaction—that is, the feeling that a product or service has met the customer expectation."[7]

Are you noticing anything common to these definitions? There is "time of sale, and thereafter." Then there is "satisfaction with a product or service" and "while performing a transaction . . . such as a sale . . ." These are all transactional definitions, and they assume—indeed, kick in—only when the customer is, presumably, about to hand over some money.

With its focus on excellence, BizWatch Online takes a slightly different approach: "Excellent customer service is the process by which your organization delivers its services or products in a way that allows the customer to access them in the most efficient, fair, cost effective, and humanly satisfying and pleasurable manner possible."[8] Still, though, it is linked to a transaction. So far, we haven't seen a word about a customer *relationship*, let alone one that can last a lifetime.

When your customers are in 1080 high-definition, you will have transactions with them, of course. But it is not those transactions that will guide how you organize to interact with your customers and how the interactions actually unfold. Rather, it will be the relationships you build with your customers, which will be built on the three 360 elements of 1080, data, intent, and processes, along with the overarching objective of enhancing the customer *experience*. To get there, you have no choice but to throw out every transaction-centered definition of what customer service is. In fact, you need to drop the antiquated idea of customer "service" altogether.

That is what American Express did, taking its organization through a transformation of its old customer service model and emerging with redefined roles for its Customer Service Representatives. Those who embraced the change, along with new hires, became Customer Care Professionals responsible for customer *engagement*. Traditional, entrenched, backward-thinking customer service reps who could not make the shift to doing business in the new way need not apply.

Consider the difference between those two words, service and engagement. Let's focus on their verb forms. To *engage* is to occupy, attract, or involve someone's interest or attention; or to cause someone to become involved in something, such as a conversation or discussion or relationship. Many of us were *engaged* to (with) our future spouses. *Engagement* is a word of relationship.

By contrast, to *service* (in the customer service context) is to perform business functions that are auxiliary to production or distribution of something. That is not a word of relationship.

American Express set out to change its interactions with customers from service to engagement, a people business that builds relationships. The transformation began with an operating framework based on what Jim Bush, executive vice president of World Service for AmEx, calls a simple concept: enable, engage, and empower. The enable part has been to create a global, integrated delivery of a promise to customers that their experience with American Express will be superb, and fulfill that promise by leveraging technology, people inside the company, and their passion. It was, and continues to be a challenge to get everyone on the same page, especially to understand that the old silo view of customer service had to be abandoned in favor of something that fits with the wholistic approach.

Engage means putting the customer first and understanding *how* to engage. As Bush tells it, this is all about listening to the customer's voice and changing the business model for American Express to reflect what the customer is saying. The new measure for the company became the straightforward Net Promoter question: "Would you recommend American Express to a friend?"

The Net Promoter question comes from Fred Reichheld, as recently described in his book *The Ultimate Question 2.0*.[9] Reichheld details how some customers are promoters and others are detractors. An American Express customer who answers a 9 or 10 to the question above is a promoter.

Several industries have dismally low average "Net Promoter Scores," a sign to me of the profound failure of companies to deal well with customers across the board, and particularly with younger customers from whom they face the wrath of an outright revolt against the old ways of doing business. In descending order, from bad to worse, these industries are cellular phone service, banks, airlines, credit cards, life insurance, health insurance, Internet, cable, and satellite TV. Those last three have *negative* scores. American Express was determined not to be among those failures.

The third part of Jim Bush's operating framework, empower, is about unleashing the abilities of American Express people who are in direct contact with customers to connect and build relationships. The company figured out how to unleash the personalities of their people, to let them be themselves, and make that come through with customers so that engagement was something real, something person-to-person and not customer-to-service rep. This wasn't easy, and American Express had to change its recruitment model for its Customer Care Professionals. Focused around the concept of extraordinary service, American Express cycled out "bad-attitude" customer service reps, recruiting "hospitable" people, changing compensation, and rewarding people not on the old-fashioned metric of average handle time, but on a new concept Bush calls "customer handling time." He defines it as an amount of time the customer dictates, based on what the customer wants and needs. That, ultimately, drives customer satisfaction. The training of Customer Care Professionals changed, too. What had once been 70 to 80 percent of training spent on technical stuff flipped completely to 70 to 80 percent spent on how to treat people and engage with customers as individuals. All of this has enabled American Express to live by its own golden rule: Treat the customer as you would like to be treated.

REWIRE THE CFO FUNCTION

One of the most significant changes your organization needs to make has to do with your chief financial officer. That's because transforming an entire organization, creating a new relationship between business and IT, and bringing your customers into high-definition is going to require making investments in people and technology. That is going to catch the attention of your chief financial officer—as well it should. The CFO is going to ask the traditional finance questions about return on investment: How long does it take? How much does it cost? What exactly are we getting for that money?

There is nothing intrinsically wrong with these questions, but the measures a CFO typically uses to answer them are problematic. How so? The CFO mind-set is traditionally linked to the way waterfall development unfolds and how the portfolio management process is used, as described in Chapter 5. That means the CFO treats building software and using technology as if you were building a huge house. You typically cannot move in and get a certificate of occupancy, until the entire house is completed. But when you are architecting pieces of a good system, with businesspeople and IT people collaborating to meet business needs, you should be able to build those pieces to deploy one room at a time.

That is completely foreign to the way the CFO typically sees capital investments and, thus, to the questions the CFO asks. The CFO wants to know the entire plan up front, which in the traditional development process may actually mean after 20 to 30 percent of the project costs have already been incurred. Typically, organizations use seed funding or have IT people do things off the books to get to a point where they can answer the questions in a way the CFO can accept. All this can end up reinforcing the waterfall approach precisely because the additional preparation makes it more likely the project will survive the gauntlet of the portfolio management process.

If you abandon the waterfall model and the portfolio management process, you also have to change how you measure the investment and potential return. Otherwise, the answers the CFO gets are not going to bode well for moving forward.

The solution lies in changing the CFO's perspective. Instead of insisting on all the facts up front, CFOs need to see that the path to monitoring the investment in business technology involves making directionally correct decisions supplemented with feedback loops and investments validated by intermediate results. In other words, keep track of the financial side, but recognize that businesspeople are going to live in some rooms before the house is finished and that they may even redecorate those rooms along the way.

It can be done. But many parts of the organization will need to collaborate to move your CFO to this new perspective. What does the CFO need to do? He or she needs to go from today's highly planned model for making decisions about technology investments to a model that is more iterative and experientially based, wherever that makes sense. It is periodic close-order inspection as an alternative to heavy planning. The CFO also needs to accept development projects being done in a way that makes them easy to launch with methods to determine what the project's real capabilities are before full commitments are made. This means a change in the mind-set about hurdle rates and return-on-investment calculations, and a culture ready to embrace a level of risk and possessed of an ability to snuff out initiatives that are not working.

A radical model for this comes to us from Janette Sadik-Khan, a commissioner of the New York City Department of Transportation who was previously senior vice president at the engineering firm Parsons Brinckerhoff. Her current work focuses on the design of cities and city streets. In an article for *Bloomberg Businessweek*, Sadik-Khan described the kind of empirical, experiential approach advocated here.

"One of our greatest innovations is our ability to move quickly. The normal capital construction program takes about five years. But we've been able to transform city streets virtually overnight. You can literally paint the city you want to see. You can do it with two traffic cones, a can of paint, and stone planters. And we're able to show the results."[10]

Imagine the ability to do that with systems for your up-and-coming Gen D customers.

It *is* possible. With tight interval control, you and your CFO can get the assurances that outcomes of a given development project will be good or that it can be stopped before everyone is too far into it. Of course, it will make a big difference if the technology being developed is, first and foremost, a way to optimize the customer experience and intelligently automate operations. If the CFO has been converted to the concept of transforming from traditional IT approaches to agile business technology, this will be much, much easier.

There is good news coming on this front. Increasingly, CFOs are becoming thought leaders in organizations. This is reinforced by a growing number of operational people being named CFOs rather than old-school accountants and finance people. More big companies have CFOs with operating experience than ever before.

That means CFOs are bringing a different skill set to the table. They can take that skill set and put it to use to change the way the systems development cycle begins. This may be more important than anything the chief information officer might do in this regard.

Remember, though, every action described in the previous chapters is intended as part of an *overall* revolutionary change in your company and how you think about your customers. None of these steps can be taken apart from the others. "Reinventing your company will not be like a makeover that involves largely cosmetic changes; it is not just about upgrading your marketing with better digital skills, or altering your go-to-market approach to exploit cheaper interactive channels, or adopting a new set of engineering disciplines for co-creating products with influential customers."[11]

What can make all this revolutionary change possible is the subject of our final chapter.

7

You Are Your Software—The Digital Imperative

The first chapter of this book posed a set of questions:

- Is your company prepared for the demographic reality barreling down on you like a runaway train, driven by new digital thinking and technologies?
- Is your company prepared for the Gen D future, or is it heading toward life support?
- Are you ready to make dramatic changes in how you think about customers and customer engagement to ensure the continuity of your business?
- Will you commit to doing everything necessary to keep customers from hating your business and some from possibly trying to kill it?

In the examples from Prudential, American Express, OCBC, and other companies, you have seen bits and pieces, some of them very large, of the changes businesses are making as they prepare for Gen D. The examples illustrate how a fundamental shift in the mind-set about how technology must support business, coupled with the 1080 high-definition customer view made possible by the data-intent-customer process combination, is the start of the path to staying alive.

The companies you have read about are letting the business drive the technology agenda. They are empowering businesspeople in their organizations and repositioning technology to serve customer interests. None of them have completely transformed every aspect of what they do to prepare for the new Gen D world, but they are probably way ahead of your business.

In Chapter 3, you read about OCBC's intent-driven process for engaging customers in opening new accounts. As exemplary as that may be, it is still old school from a Gen D perspective. But OCBC has a very clear picture of the Gen D train barreling down the tracks. So, OCBC has introduced FRANK.

Mind you, OCBC is not some inherently cool banking upstart. It is a $200 billion financial institution that already controls more than a quarter of the total youth market in Singapore. But the company is committed to locking in Gen D customers by doing business in a way that doesn't seem like marketing, instead letting customers *discover* the bank.

The FRANK name comes from the phrase "frankly speaking," a reflection of OCBC's understanding that Gen D expects honesty, transparency, and sincerity. The brick-and-mortar FRANK stores—and they are stores, not what you typically think of as bank branches—seem to have been modeled after the Apple Store. Young people are drawn into the stores, which are located in malls where Gen D hangs out. The objective of the store design is to encourage customers to browse, touch, and ask questions. Yes, touch, just as if you were shopping for clothes or some kind of gadget.

The FRANK Website looks like the Website for Virgin Mobile, a cell phone provider geared to young customers, but with anything looking business-like stripped down to the bare essentials.[1] The bank made a conscious decision to omit anything even remotely superfluous. For instance, there isn't even the ubiquitous link to an "About Us" page. Products are minimal, and cross-promotion is king. Apply for a tuition loan and you get a gift voucher for the movies. Open a checking account and you get a laptop sleeve. If you can convince four friends to sign up for FRANK products, you'll all share in $50 worth of Ben & Jerry's ice cream.

OCBC offers higher-than-normal interest rates to FRANK customers who open savings accounts and fuels their loyalty with a "savings enabler" tool that allows them to create subaccounts in the form of "savings jars" that they name themselves, just like putting change into a jar at home. And that money cannot be accessed through an ATM.

Other banks are leveraging digital technologies in unique ways to improve the customer experiences, too, though at this writing OCBC seems to be the one most focused on Gen D. For instance, Commonwealth Bank of Australia has a smartphone app that "changes the house-hunting experience. A prospective home buyer begins by taking a picture of a house he or she likes. Using image-recognition software and location-based technologies, the app identifies the house and provides the list price, taxes, and other information. It then connects with the buyer's personal financial data and (with further links to lender databases) determines whether the buyer can be preapproved for a mortgage (and, if so, in what amount). This nearly instantaneous series of interactions cuts through the hassle of searching real-estate agents' sites for houses and then connecting with the agents or with mortgage brokers for financing, which might take a week."[2]

You can be sure the users of this app are not being followed around on their smartphones by some real estate agent's advertisement. And with ubiquitous digital technology, by the time young Gen D members are ready to buy homes they may be able to take a picture of a house that isn't even for sale and have one found that matches. Talk about seamless!

CORE PRINCIPLES FOR SURVIVAL

How did OCBC get to the point where the company could see clearly down those tracks and know what to do to prepare? The bank has been working on liberating its organization, just as described in Chapter 6, and it has changed the way businesspeople and technology people interact in the organization. OCBC is also putting technology to use in a new way, which, when teased apart, reveals three core principles that make feasible everything you've read about up to this point.

1. Democratize how you do technology.
2. Think in layers.
3. Use analytics to optimize continually.

Each principal has a business component and a technology component, but is fundamentally about making technology empower and serve the businesspeople in your organization. Technology is at the center of your ability to respond to the Gen D threat and the Gen D opportunity.

DEMOCRATIZE HOW YOU DO TECHNOLOGY

When people first began to create documents, it was an arduous and individual task that involved chiseling stone. Eventually, that gave way to writing on parchment. The individual nature of the process changed when groups of scribes collaborated to create great tomes, usually of religious works. Along came the printing press, a new, disruptive technology that democratized the creation and dissemination of documents by making it possible for you to hand over what you wrote in longhand to someone who could mass produce copies.

Much later, further democratization was achieved when the typewriter came along. Individual writers shifted to the new technology. Large companies created huge typing pools, often floors and floors of mostly women who would type up handwritten notes from the men of the company or turn Dictaphone loops into documents.

When the mimeograph was introduced, individuals could mass produce copies of their own documents without handing it over to a trained printer. Again, we were all pushed further along on the democratization spectrum. Then, when Wang Laboratories perfected dedicated word processing computers, all those typing scribes were empowered with another new, and very powerful, technology.

The next step in democratization, the personal computer, arrived. It directly empowered people at all levels to take direct control—wiping out the typing pools. And now with tablets becoming ubiquitous, the digital lifecycle of concept to creation to specialization to consumption to feedback runs full circle.

Now, information technology has caught up with writing and publishing—empowering changed relationships between business and IT and unleashing a new wave of automation. Not only is *access* to technology more democratic, but there now exists the ability to shift the control of, responsibility over, and accountability for technology away from dedicated gurus and experts with some mysterious and impenetrable skill set to businesspeople operating more centrally within their domain of knowledge and using the language and metaphors of business to guide how technology gets used. It is a complete transformation from IT driving the use of technology to businesspeople driving its use and evolution.

In simple terms, this means you, the businessperson, no longer need visit the technology wizard to make a simple, but important change to a business system, even something as straightforward as making it a bit easier to use. After all, typical software engineers do not consider the nuances of how fields are organized on the screen

to be their domain. They are not particularly interested in eliminating clicks or addressing the work-specific details that are so critical to
businesspeople. Democratization makes it so the wizards only need
to engage in specialized circumstances, leaving them to concentrate
on where they can add the greatest value implementing the most
technically complex interfaces or extreme systems for analysis or
transaction execution. This creates a parallel with the current state of
word processing, where nearly all of it can be done by businesspeople
themselves, and the wizards—in this case, professional designers and
creative document experts—are only needed for certain specialties.

Democratizing how we do technology means dramatically shifting the power base within your organization. It is about getting rid
of technology language in favor of business language and actuating
organizational liberation. Businesspeople no longer need technology
translators. Today's powerful computers make it possible to move
from having to use machine language to being able to use business
language concepts directly in structured yet readily understand-
able business language. And if a computer can be programmed with
direct business language, it stands to reason that a businessperson
can do that work directly, eliminating the delays, murkiness, and mis-
understanding that can occur when translation must be done.

This makes sense from the perspectives of efficiency and effectiveness.
An advantage of democratizing technology is that if you give the people
who care most about certain aspects of anything the ability to deal with
those aspects themselves, they are likely to do the best job. Leave any
elements that are highly technical, such as complicated system interfaces, to the technologists, and move the vast majority of the work and
control to the businesspeople, and the implementation and ongoing
improvement of technology solutions will be both faster and better.

THINK IN LAYERS

What happens when you have empowered your businesspeople
to drive technology, not the other way around, is that they themselves can build solutions that are much more likely to correspond
to the real needs of your customers. The technologists who have

been creating your systems have been coerced by the tool sets they use to create systems that are flat. These systems, because they are constrained by the rigid computer codes and language described in Chapter 5, live in a world of only two dimensions. Indeed, they are typically represented as some type of flow chart captured on a two-dimensional page, with choices and alternatives reflected as so-called "if-then-else" branches shown on the flat diagram.

However, your business has *more* logic and choice than can be readily captured this way and, indeed, has multiple aspects and dimensions. Business problems, decisions, issues, processes, and customers are multidimensional. And your nascent Gen D customers will have layers of situation, circumstance, and context that are exponentially more complex than we can even imagine now.

Looking across industries, it becomes apparent that nearly all differences within a given business fall within a fairly consistent set of dimensions. They are *customers, products*, and *jurisdictions*. Customers may be of different types. Products fall into different categories. Jurisdictions—some are geographic, while others may be channels—impose all sorts of variations, from different rules and regulations to culture-driven ways of doing business and dealing with customers.

This brings us to the second core principle: think in layers. First and foremost, layers require that your technology be able to work across all three dimensions, which likely include not only multiple customers but also multiple products and jurisdictions, in ways that correspond to the multitudinous facets of your customers. Fail to think in layers, and the customer experience on the phone will diverge inappropriately from the customer experience on the Web, and so on. Gen C customers notice that. Gen D customers will never stand for it.

The binary, if-then, flat systems you now have create some very bad choices for you when you try to think in the rich multidimensional world of your customer. Actually, bad does not even come close—the choices are *horrible*.

Imagine you are a bank with a system that can write loans in North America, where there are particular rules and regulations, customer types, and even business intent specific to that part of the world. You expand to England, and you want to use that same system to write loans there. But wait! That system has all sorts of manual connections linked to specifically North American criteria. So, to adapt the system, you need to look at all of its 500-plus system modules and then manually identify the 35 or so that need to be changed in some way.

Here is your first horrible choice: make each of those separate modules more complicated so they can handle both North America and England. You do this by creating new code branches, using if-then-else constructs. This creates an unsustainable and ever-growing mass of many little embedded decisions for the system to use to differentiate effectively between North America and England.

You have created a monster. The differences between North America and England are now buried across 35 modules. What happens when your bank expands to Spain and Portugal? The conditionalization becomes more and more complex, until you get to the point where it is very dangerous to make changes. For instance, you might create the very real possibility that when your success leads to opening branches in Brazil, making changes to accommodate that new business opportunity could break the system for use in England. That's because everything is linked together into a horrible series of decisions buried invisibly in the programming that makes no real sense from an outside-in point of view.

The second, even more horrible, choice involves copying the original 35 system modules and then changing or deleting whatever you need to so they work for England. The advantage is that now England and North America have exactly what they need. There's no extra overhead, and no extra processing, but neither is there any sharing. And again, the differences are spread across 35 modules. You have two versions of the same underlying piece of code that are probably no more than 5 percent different. What happens when you expand again, and eventually you have done this seven more times? Maybe it is a different 5 percent that needs to change. Will you ever be able to find all the relevant things to change? Not to mention that you have to test the other 95 percent in every version of the system to make sure you haven't introduced any new problems. And if something fundamental needs to change, suddenly you need to position that common characteristic in each of the copies—an expensive and risky endeavor.

With either choice, the next thing you know is that your system is a massive, unsupportable mess. In fact, you have multiple messes—called "versions." Want to find out what's different about the processing in Germany? Forget it, unless you are willing to devote a lot of resources to scouring all of the incredibly messy modules.

Both of these choices lead to zombie systems, and it is common to hear both business and IT people say they simply do not know the details of what the systems actually do. Those zombie systems encourage manual systems and rogue systems, because businesspeople need to get their work done.

The critically necessary alternative is to think in layers. Identify what is common and what is distinctive. Figure out the degrees of difference. Tell the computer, in simple terms, what you've found. The modern computer, fully capable of fulfilling this function for you, can then simply give you the multidimensional technology tooling you need. Thinking in layers makes it possible to achieve the most genuine personalization possible for every customer's engagement with you by respecting the customer's context in terms of what is similar and what is different. If you want to allow Gen D to get the sense of discovery its members crave, you absolutely must be able to personalize this way.

Once you have gotten past the restraints of traditional programming language and you have empowered businesspeople by democratizing how you do technology, thinking in layers becomes easier. You can build systems with layers that eliminate the horrible choices. It will be as easy as having businesspeople simply specify what is different between North America and England and let the computer do the rest. The businesspeople will be able to make simple adjustments for a particular customer or class of customers, particular products, particular geographies, particular channels . . . you name it.

Today's computers will take care of the rest. They are fully capable of writing their own code, based on more advanced metaphors that incorporate business intent and business process. Software can now understand what businesspeople have to say, in their own language, and can go directly from model to an actual, usable system with full functionality. You bypass the arcane practice of coding and instead focus directly on what your businesspeople need.

A useful, if simplistic visualization, for this layered approach comes from the world of digital media and the way in which designers use composite layers to create different versions of images and movies. Designers can choose what is unique and specific, without sacrificing inheritance from their parent layers. Different layers can be turned off and on within the same artwork to create different results for different purposes. Today's digital artists, unlike today's computer software programmers, do not need to make multiple "branched" versions of a file that force them to create completely new versions manually.

In the following Adobe Photoshop example, the designer has deselected the eyeball on the left so that the U.S. and U.K. layers and bronze customers will not show up in this composite—just the ones

we want for our purposes at the moment, only the gold customers in Canada. Our business systems should be this easy.

Unfortunately, the problem of *not* thinking in layers is endemic across the computing landscape. It isn't being addressed in the Shadow IT organizations, and does not go away when you move to the cloud. Businesses using the cloud still remain dependent on the technologists for any significant changes to the solutions themselves. Someone *still* has to write code to make business logic changes to reflect new products, new procedures, new regulations and new customer behaviors. But code is the status quo and that means code just gets in the way of efficient business.

The good news is there is simply no longer a need to rely on writing code. Businesspeople today can illustrate their processes, think in layers, set their goals, and then state unequivocally to the computer what constitutes a proper outcome. Then they can let the computer write (and, as necessary, rewrite) the code.

USE ANALYTICS TO OPTIMIZE CONTINUALLY

Once you have begun to think in layers, across many dimensions, and your technology thinks the same way, you can further empower your businesspeople so they can continuously refine your high-definition view of customers. This is critical preparation for the coming Gen D customerpocalypse. Analytics allow you to validate and further tease apart the dimensionality, bringing intent and responsiveness to your multidimensional thinking. Analytics help you determine whether you have identified the right dimensions for the right customers. From analytics, you get extra insight.

Chapter 3 described the approach called *next-best-action* that allows you to use advanced analytics to examine trends and patterns across millions of customers. These dynamic analytics are a way to sense customer needs, choices, preferences, and how to anticipate behavior. And they are at the heart of the third core principle for achieving genuine business technology.

Dynamic analytics are a prerequisite to keeping your customer in sharp focus. During an interaction with a customer, you or the customer can provide new data that can dynamically change the results from the underlying predictive model. Imagine a customer interacting with a financial institution, and the institution finds out during the interaction that the customer has just inherited $500,000 from a deceased relative. This would dramatically change the risk score of the customer and how you want, very respectfully, to engage with that customer. The system adapts so that the customer's choices change to whatever the institution has decided in advance is more appropriate for a customer fitting the new profile. In other words, dynamic analytics make that intent 360 possible.

But it is also goes beyond the data—the very path through the system provides input to the customer's level of interest. This is as true in a guided interaction (say, with a contact center) as it is in looking at how a customer navigates a Website during self-service.

Humans adapt to other humans all the time, in real time. That is the very nature of human interaction, as information is provided back and forth between two or more people. Why shouldn't technology do the same?

Rob Walker, the colleague who provided the C.C. Sabathia baseball analogy in Chapter 3, imagined unleashing predictive, dynamic analytics on health care data. Consider just a few of his examples of how it might be used in that domain, and then imagine how powerful it would be in getting to true business technology. He suggests its employment to predict the duration of operations, pre- and postoperative complications from surgery, transplant rejection, complications in newborn babies, and so on. In the case of predicting postoperative atrial arrhythmia, the tool would identify when and which additional medications are necessary during procedures to ensure better outcomes. He also showed how scheduling based on predictive duration of operations would eliminate at least 14 percent of the downtime in operating rooms. For the average hospital, that amounts to millions of dollars and thousands of improved patient outcomes each year.

As PNC Bank's Chief Marketing Officer Karen Larrimer explains, "Analytics is all about the science, there's tons of power in what we can do today with science . . . But if you don't combine it with the right art in the customer experience, that science won't be as useful. Data is extremely important and it's at the core of everything we're doing. But it is not about the data, it's about the insight. Big data is useless if it's just a bunch of data you can't turn into insight."[3]

In essence, this principle underlying genuine business technology is about getting past assumptions and averages to achieve a much clearer picture of the customer based on higher-level science. It is about empowering systems that are capable of adapting, by using data and outcomes so that they can offer feedback directly into the business intent of an enterprise and recommend changes in real time.

These three principles are the basis for staying alive today and living to see another day with Gen D.

FROM DREAM TO REALITY

Democratize how you do technology. Insist on using the language of business, not the programming language of the machines, and let businesspeople understand how to speak directly to what they want accomplished. Use technology that can generate code on its own, based on that business language. Think in layers. Marry data and intent in processes that are for the customer, so the customer experience is seamless and corresponds to what Gen D expects and demands. Harness the power of analytics to support what you are doing for customers. Make sure those systems are built to change, not to become dinosaurs that compel businesspeople to go rogue. Embrace collaboration. Support reuse.

These are the steps to genuine business technology. They address some of the reasons that in a growing number of enterprises, the marketing function is eclipsing the IT function in technology spending. And they go even further.

George Colony, the founder and CEO of Forrester Research, has been touting a shift from information technology to business technology and from technologist to businessperson for quite some time. It "is taking longer than expected," reported *CIO* magazine back in 2009.[4]

Still, Colony has surely been on to something. "Changing the term to BT," he told *CIO* magazine back then, "is also a powerful way for the chief technologist—CIO or CTO—to signal to line-of-business managers and executives and also to the presidents, COO, CEO, and the board of directors that 'We're not in the technology business anymore; we're in the real business—the company's business.' I believe by changing the name to BT, and changing its behavior to focus on the business of the business, the technology organization would transform its relationship with the business. I think it would begin to communicate in a different language (the language of business), the current lack of communication would dissipate, and we'd have a higher level of communication around the business problems and the business issues. Which, of course, the presidents and line execs think and care about every day, but all too often, the technologists don't. Changing the name from IT to BT is a way to change the mind-set in IT and change the relationship between technologies and businesspeople. Definitely."

Colony is correct, but without the underlying principles discussed here, the dream of achieving true business technology will remain a dream. Without capturing the underlying concepts that represent and govern how the business works or should work, and capturing them in the language of the businesspeople themselves, systems will continue to fail the businesspeople who use them. The time is now.

The Forrester call to arms around the business technology concept was first introduced near the end of the last decade. Finally, in the business world, the idea is showing some serious traction and adoption. And as that has happened, the Forrester analysts have clarified the concept and strengthened the specific context of the "age of the customer."

Business technology, writes Peter Burris, "must become a customer-facing function." That should sound familiar to readers of this book. "Emerging technologies can capture and apply customer insights to serve customers in their moment of need. Digital technologies are improving offerings and streamlining engagement through new digital touchpoints. As technology's importance in customer experience rises, BT should focus on what customers want and how to deliver it."[5]

Further, writes Burris, companies need to "design systems of engagement" with their customers. "Business should regard customer engagement holistically, factoring in the interplay of customer-facing technologies and employees, different channels, suites of offerings, and customer contexts. Create systems of engagements from the outside in, from customer moments of need back to systems of record."

That is the right direction. However, without the layering that enables multidimensionality and that gives people systems that work both up and down and sideways, systems will fail businesspeople and never become business technology. Absent capturing the commonalities across silos and channels, and having processes that merge customer data with customer and business intent, the unified and enhanced customer experience that businesspeople absolutely must be prepared to provide to Gen D will remain a dream.

And without an automation capability by and for businesspeople, the business technology objective will remain an elusive one. Anything and everything that can be automated for greater effect should be automated, and the automation has to be so simple and based on business-friendly metaphors so that no specially trained translator is required to create the computer code needed to do the job.

What makes all this possible is the overall model for business technology as we head into the future. It is about ending the reign of two-dimensional systems that do not serve the interest of achieving 1080 customer high-definition. It is about blueprints that can build themselves. It is about technology that actually makes it possible to end the relationship between business and IT based on a master craftsman. No more will you need to get an expert to design for you, and then hire a craftsman to create an example of what you want, and then contract with manufacturers to create the finished product. Those days—and those kinds of IT roles—can and will come to an end.

Something else will come to an end, too: a certain *insanity* that permeates the software industry. In just about every industry except for software, there is an understanding of the need to go from concept to execution. That understanding got us to computer-aided design and computer-aided manufacturing (CAD/CAM). In so many fields today, computer systems are used to help create, modify, analyze, or optimize designs. Architects design buildings using CAD/CAM. Industrial engineers create all manner of widgets using CAD/CAM. It is the digitalization of the physical world, and everyone gets it. In the physical world, technology has advanced to the point where we are even on the cusp of linking design directly to delivery. We can now create physical models that can be customized and manufactured individually, coming to life in real time through a new generation of 3D printers. There is a seamless connection between standard design, personalization, and execution.

Given that fact, it is rather ironic that information technology powers CAD/CAM and that computers aid in the design of just about everything *except computer software*! Think about how powerful it is to apply these same concepts to how businesspeople will shape the ways in which your information technology systems get built.

GROWING PRESSURE

The pressure to make these kinds of changes is not going away. It is only going to get more intense, more relentless.

Consider the findings released in late 2013 by Accenture, the consulting firm introduced in Chapter 5. The firm summarizes these findings from its "2013 Global Consumer Pulse Survey" in a fascinating infographic available to anyone.[6] In many respects, the summary reads like a play-by-play analysis for how Gen D is already affecting your company.

First, there is the reference to the "demands of a more dynamic empowered consumer" (Gen D being the up-and-coming component). This group puts "at play" a "revenue potential of up to $5.9 trillion." Why "at play"? Some 66 percent of these consumers "switched companies in at least one of ten industries due to poor service the past year," and 82 percent "felt their provider could have done something to prevent them from switching."

Meanwhile, "digital adoption continues to rise," and "mobile online access accelerates the trend." Some 89 percent use at least one online channel, and the average is *three* digital channels—with close to 40 percent using a mobile device for access at least half the time.

But perhaps most telling is that 51 percent of U.S. customers "have much higher expectations of getting specialized treatment for being a 'good' customer" than in the previous year. Have you figured out how to offer "specialized treatment" to a customer who does not want to be sold to? Gen D members want you to make them *discover* that they're special!

The executive summary of the Accenture report goes into even more detail and highlights just how critical it is to adopt a new way of thinking and the technology to make it possible to do business in a new way. For instance, "Word-of-mouth, including that shared via social media, continues to be the most important and impactful source of company information across industries and is used by 71 percent of surveyed customers."[7]

There is a very large gap to close. "The gap between the use of digital technologies and the ability of companies to use them to improve customer experiences is highlighted by the survey's findings that, among the 10 industries covered by the report, none made noticeable progress in providing customers with a tailored experience in 2013. In the utilities industry, only 18 percent of customers agreed their provider offered them a tailored experience. And even in industries such as hotels and lodging and retail banking, perceived to be leading in creating more personalized interactions, only 36 percent of customers acknowledge receiving a tailored experience, respectively."

That bears repeating: ". . . none made noticeable progress . . ." In a nutshell, says Accenture, "[O]ur survey of more than 12,800 consumers in 32 countries tells us companies' efforts are falling short . . ."

Of course, Accenture and Forrester are not *literally* saying that the sky is falling. Still, you can deny the facts of the overall customerpocalypse climate change only at your own risk. Your company's world *is* changing. Gen D is the ascending protagonist in Forrester's "age of the customer." Gen D will soon be at the switch in what Accenture calls the "switching economy."[8]

There are tremendously compelling reasons to act before the Achilles' heel of most companies overtakes your ability to correct your course and be ready for Gen D barreling down the pike. That Achilles' heel is the woefully poor job technology providers have done in truly empowering businesses to innovate and differentiate when it comes to how they engage with customers.

Technology providers seem to spend so much of their time telling stories and so much of their money investing in promoting marketing visions of the future (e.g., "smarter planets"). That's in lieu of delivering real empowerment. It's almost like a classic shell game on a table out on a city street, but with six shells. One is labeled "social," another "Big Data," and the other four are "outsourcing," "the cloud," "in-memory predictive analytics," and "mobile." The technology providers hope that if they shuffle the shells around the table quickly enough, you won't be able to remember under which one they placed the empowerment and profit "pea"—if there's one at all.

There's nothing inherently wrong with any of those shells. Indeed, they each have tremendous potential—if they were to be applied in the right context and under the control of the businesspeople. The big problem is that not a single one of them is *you*—what you know about your markets, your customers, your products, your methods, your best policies, the strengths and weaknesses of your organization, as well as those of your competition. Your *intent* and your customers' *intent* are missing, too. And at least one of them, "the cloud," is meant to reinforce the notion that software has become irrelevant thanks to a "big switch."[9]

You are not going to get all that missing *you* into your systems and processes through any or all of what is under the shells. You need to embrace and celebrate systems and processes that get your digital DNA into scalable technology that allows for respectful customer engagement and competitive differentiation. You need that combination of brains and brawn that makes you agile, that enables you to sense and respond successfully (as described in Chapter 4). And you need to be in a position to drive sustainable change in how your business executes.

All this leads to something that may seem quite counterintuitive: the companies that will not only survive the customerpocalypse but that will thrive with Gen D *will, in a sense, themselves become software companies.*

This idea flows directly from an observation made by Marc Andreessen, one of the world's leading information technology wizards. He pioneered the Web browser as a co-creator of Mosaic, co-founded Netscape, and has since become a titan among technology venture capitalists and is a prominent thinker about the future. In a 2011 article in the *Wall Street Journal*, he argued that despite how we may see the following companies, every one of the them (and quite a few others not listed here) is actually a software company: Amazon, Netflix, iTunes, Spotify, Pandora, Groupon, Skype (the world's fastest growing telecom company), AT&T and Verizon (which "have survived by transforming themselves into software companies, partnering with Apple and other smartphone makers"), LinkedIn ("today's fastest growing recruiting company") . . . and the list goes on.[10]

Andreessen's conclusion: "Software is eating the world." What he means is that "we are in the middle of a dramatic and broad technological and economic shift in which software companies are poised to take over large swathes of the economy."

If Andreessen is right, then you really do need to become a software company to survive the coming customerpocalypse. "Companies in every industry," he writes, "need to assume that a software revolution is coming. This includes even industries that are software-based today . . . Over the next 10 years, the battles between incumbents and software-powered insurgents will be epic. Joseph Schumpeter, the economist who coined the term 'creative destruction,' would be proud."

What will it look like to become a software company? The company's businesspeople will be fully engaged in creating the systems and processes (the software) that powers their survival and thriving. Just as supply chain matters, just as logistics matters, so, too, do you need software that is *you*, that is *your brand promise*, your *company DNA*, your *code of ethics*, and your *authentic customer commitment*.

In the online global economy, in a world of the ascendant Gen D, your software as described here is how your customers will touch you and test you.

Is that something you want to leave to some technology provider? Or would you rather have your organization do it, tapping into the power of your businesspeople and your technologists working together in a new kind of collaboration? Chances are, that technology provider is going to try to sell you on something dumbed down, or reduced to a placebo app that promises immediate ease-of-use and gratification but that ultimately fails to deliver. It certainly won't contain your digital DNA. That's something you and your organization have to define, shape, evolve, and communicate.

Today, more than ever before, if you want to face up to the realities of the coming Gen D you need to learn from Amazon, Google, and other companies that understand that technology systems of customer engagement are more critical than systems of operational management have ever been.

In short, this is on you. There is no silver bullet. You'll need all the shells on the technology providers' card table, but need to be able to apply them in the spirit of a digital and democratized enterprise. And what you will need even more is the realization that your customers, especially those coming Gen D customers, will judge you or embrace you based on how you "feel" to them when they touch you. If your epidermal software skin is sensitive, responsive, authentic, and aware of their context, and if it is alert and respectful of their intentions, they will embrace you. If they sense you are hiding behind your technology, like a defensive shield, they will judge you to be not worthy of engagement.

As Andreessen writes, the new software companies will "need to prove their worth. They need to build strong cultures, delight their customers, establish their own competitive advantages and, yes, justify their rising valuations. No one should expect building a new high-growth, software-powered company in an established industry to be easy. It's brutally difficult."

There are no packaged applications that will do this for you. The old-school software systems—typically clumsy and monolithic lumps of technology like the plethora of enterprise resource planning systems grinding away in the back rooms of the world's companies—suffer from a hopeless lack of agility, and the efforts to make them responsive is a big part of the company disaster stories you have read about in this book.

And there is no app for that. There are none of those cute little programs designed to do very specific things and work on your smartphone or tablet. Sure, many of today's ubiquitous apps have lots of admirable attributes. Apps are great for doing very specific things. They offer ease of use and often deliver genuine delight to customers. But in terms of the future survival of your company, you need to ask whether they represent the core of how customer engagement and efficient operations will evolve.

Any company that thinks it will overcome the challenge of engaging successfully with Gen D and ensuring its survival by creating even the greatest one-off mobile apps is in big trouble. Apps are not omnichannel, but are intrinsically siloed. For any multichannel business, no app can possibly represent the totality of your digital DNA, your company's *you*-ness. They are most certainly *not* the technology foundation on which to build broad, long-term customer engagement and experiences with Gen D. At best, an app is one small tactic, not a strategy.

If, however, you can capture your commitment to customers, to the ascendant Gen D, in your customer processes and in your own software systems that execute that commitment, you can succeed and survive to build competitive advantage.

Surely you can sense that there is a lot of antipathy in the business community for the legacy baggage of traditional computer programming. Nothing could be more critical than to get the technologists doing what only they can do, and let the businesspeople make their computers and systems work the way they need them to work. The "switching economy" is now; it's not going to wait for you to catch up. If the argument in this book has been particularly hard on the guild culture of writing software code by hand, stressing the importance of eliminating the classic trap of writing requirements for an illusory future to-be state, it's because we're facing a customerpocalypse! You can't win when the technology systems that power your engagements with customers, Gen D or otherwise, are based on requirements that are outdated the moment they were written down.

The alternative proposed in this book is that you can incorporate the digital DNA of your business into your own unique software by employing technology that learns by doing, adapts in real time, and empowers your best business thinkers to accelerate innovation.

YOUR NEXT STEPS

If you take away only one thing from this book, let it be what you read here.

First, your survival as a business depends on whether you can and are willing to change your expectations. The first set of expectations you have to change concerns your customers, both current and future. They've certainly changed their expectations about you. As you have seen, the up-and-coming Gen D does not care whether you live or die. But you can have them as customers, as long as you respond to them in ways that are unlike anything you have done before. The high-def customer experience is going to be the critical factor in maintaining and thriving in the Gen D world.

You also need to change whatever expectations you may have about the security, or insecurity, of your position in the market. Guaranteed, if you are not changing your customer expectations, you might as well decide right now to become very, very insecure going forward.

The third set of expectations you must change is about what your organization and technology can do. Technology like that described in Chapter 5, coupled with an organization that functions along the lines outlined in Chapter 7, is your salvation. It is what will get you into a conversation with Gen D and keep you alive as you try to negotiate the difficult world they are creating. Don't miss the chance.

You need to understand that it is possible to use technology in a wholly different way than you have been, and that if you do so it will fundamentally change the game. It is possible to model your business in a different way. It is possible to stop writing code. It actually is possible to build for change. But none of that will happen unless you are willing to blow up some big traditions and impediments of the status quo. And if you don't, Gen D will gleefully blow you up instead.

All of this falls under the umbrella of your business culture. Are you ready to embrace a culture that is relationship-oriented? If so, you have to smash the vestiges of the old culture that get in the way of developing relationships that are going to enhance your customers' experiences with you and, in fact, bring them joy, glee, and discovery. You have to commit fully to pragmatic, seamless experiences for your staff along with magical experiences for your customers. And that requires a cultural commitment throughout your enterprise.

More than that, it requires a leadership regime that embraces iteration, experimentation, and contained risk. No longer can you abide asking the old CFO questions that preclude discussion and change. No more can you have any kind of CIO other than one who understands that you are in the business technology business. You must have a CIO who doesn't just reach across the aisle between business and IT, but works actively to get rid of the aisle.

Industry thought leader Michael Maoz suggests the best thing you could do for your organization is to send your CIO out as an undercover customer. "Imagine if our CIOs had the opportunity to be paid to spend a year living on the front line serving the customer?," he writes. He'd like to see them using that time to learn more about the customer perspective: "[W]hat is it like to be a customer? How does the customer perceive your channel strategy? Do they live the experiences the way that you engineered them?"[11]

"Successful technology leaders," write Colony and Burris, "will have knowledge of customers and, perhaps most importantly, a passion for the work of attracting, retaining, and serving them."[12] That is so true. As the CIO of a mutual insurance company told these authors, "Our company is moving beyond the CIO to someone who can take responsibility for customer experience."

And your businesspeople, from marketing to customer service, have to understand that in this new world they not only are being given great new power, but that they have to measure their effectiveness differently, be hands on with customers at every level, and accept a new accountability for business outcomes.

There is an incredible sense of urgency to all this. The coming customerpocalypse, with Gen D leading the charge, will never be met simply by adding to your company a veneer of popular social media or by adopting the Net Promoter concept or even by instituting a great voice-of-the-customer program. No—you must address the *structural and systemic barriers* to your business survival and growth. You have to do this with the customer at the very center of your thinking, so you can survive this age of the customer. And you have to do it in what to anyone older than Gen D may seem like a world turned upside down.

The "switching economy" is a world in which consumers sometimes find themselves rewarded for disloyalty—as when a mobile phone provider pays transfer fees for those who switch, killing the illusion of customer loyalty that has been supported by the friction involved in making change happen. It is a world in which the concept of "owning" a product has changed—from the Xbox One fiasco with used games described in Chapter 1 to Spotify, Pandora, and Beats Music on the Web making it possible to rent music (for next to nothing) rather than buying it to own. Gen D does not feel the importance of owning something the way its predecessor generations have, and that changes everything.

Survival depends on *immediate* action. "It's time to play to win and stop playing not to lose."[13] The time has come to leave behind the stale organizational thinking that cripples innovation and forces CFOs to drive by looking in a rear view mirror when it comes to the technology development process. Because of what's coming, you need to ask more of technology than you ever thought possible. It absolutely, positively must all be about the customer experience. And you need to *be* authentic, not just *seem* to be authentic. You can achieve authenticity only with customer engagement that is a seamless part of your entire operational strategy.

This is a huge challenge, perhaps the greatest one your business will ever face. No one yet knows who will survive the customerpocalypse. The jury is still out for even the enterprises that have undertaken the most advanced, customer-centric examples in this book. The only thing certain is that you must change. If you fail to understand that "software is eating the world" and create the systems and software that best express your digital DNA, and if you fail to earn customers' trust by respecting their position of empowerment, you will not only fail to win over Generation D. You stand a very good chance of not even being around to try your hand with the generations that will follow.

BEYOND THE TWILIGHT OF THE BRANDS

Businesses today can and must learn from Generation D. As this book describes, these empowered customers are instantly informed about themselves (self-monitoring for physical and financial health) and the world around them (personalized news and on-demand content). They use smartphones, mobile computing, and powerful wearable devices such as contact lenses to monitor diabetic glucose levels. They routinely accept powerful shopping agents that aggregate and compare prices, and express immediate dissatisfaction through social media to demonize suppliers that disappoint them. These customers are much less amenable to traditional advertising, are more informed, and more demanding.

As James Surowiecki wrote in "Twilight of the Brands," the empowered, mobile, and instantly informed and connected consumer has upset the notion of brand loyalty, roiling the world of advertising and marketing: "For much of the twentieth century, consumer markets were stable. Today, they are tumultuous, and you're only as good as your last product."[14]

Surowiecki is correct, but he doesn't go far enough. You are also only as good as your current two-way interaction with your customer.

Look more closely, and you will see that the space in which those interactions occur is increasingly virtual. It is designed and delivered by software. Your customers will judge you by this virtual software interaction before they even look at your product. Again, this new virtual layer has matured rapidly; what was once a supporting role has become a primary means of engagement. It governs and informs everything from personalized marketing and digital advertising to your social media and Internet presence. Software is fundamental. It drives your call center and the mobile apps you give employees and consumers. It trains and guides your associates and virtual agents. It is your software that will listen, learn, and predict customer preferences. It will govern product lifecycle. It will ensure regulatory compliance, service levels, and the efficiency of your supply chain.

As it scales to massive volumes of interactions, your software will come to represent who you are as much as your carbon-based employees or brick-and-mortar locations. This is not as futuristic and science-fictionish as it may seem. Properly done, your software *is* you. It is the "you" with whom customers engage first and most. In the twilight of the brands, it can either differentiate you or make you fail. That is why it is so important to make the omnipresent and omni-channel epidermal software layer your customers use to engage with you something that *no one else could possibly make.*

The static brand identity may be in its twilight, but the always-on, constantly learning and adapting virtual software layer is taking its place because you are only as good as your current engagement. You no longer win a customer for life. You renew that trust in an endless stream of ongoing moments of truth. To be challenged continually to earn this level of trust, though, is the best thing that could happen, since the new consumer will actively advocate on your behalf in a way that passive brand fans never did.

To be sure, making this software level come alive is hard to do. At the very time we should be investing more of ourselves in our software, technology providers seem to be encouraging us to abdicate what software can do for us. The tragic flaw of software is rooted in the deep rabbit hole the software programming fraternity has dug for itself over the past 40 years: a zombie-like perpetuation of manual coding that eschews abstract modeling and declarative thinking.

Nearly a decade ago, Jeannette Wing described the problem well. "Computational thinking," she wrote, is "a fundamental skill for everyone, not just for computer scientists. To reading, writing, and arithmetic, we should add computational thinking to every child's analytical ability."[15]

Unfortunately, Wing's advice has been largely ignored. Instead, youth are being apprenticed to the craft-based guild of the Code Academy, where they are trained to pound out lines of Ruby on Rails and JSON manually, and where they have become an army of human sacrifices to feed endless volcanic eruptions of magma streams of hand-crafted JavaScript. Wing declared that the best way to deal with computers is to develop capabilities in accordance with the "way that humans, not computers, think. Computational thinking is a way humans solve problems; it is not trying to get humans to think like computers. Computers are dull and boring; humans are clever and imaginative. We humans make computers exciting."

Wing is right: if done properly, we *can* make computers exciting, and you can capture your unique cultural personalities and manifest it in the always-on brand layer. But technology providers continue to prescribe ever more manual coding, ever more digging, and the hole gets deeper and deeper. You can create a software layer that can carry on an authentic relationship with your customers effectively by abandoning or delegating authorship.

Today, many in the technology sector are falsely claiming that any number of the bright shiny objects in the following list will magically allow your business to become a "digital" organization.

- Fire your IT department and go strictly for Software as a Service in the Cloud
- Invest in-memory analytics fueled by Big Data
- Fire your IT department and send all your coding requirements offshore
- Get your advertising agency to produce a bunch of me-too mobile apps
- Hire outside integrators to build custom solutions for you on best-of-breed technologies
- Add social media icons to all of your corporate online presences
- Shift all of your ad spend to something your agency has called "digital marketing"
- Give your CEO a Twitter account
- And then hire a truckload of new staff to monitor sentiment and social response

But what is missing and what is wrong in this how-to-become-a-digital-organization laundry list is something very fundamental. Where is the advice to empower your best innovators to think about your customers' journey, first and foremost (and as described in Chapter 4), and to model that customer journey in a way *only they can*? Where are the tools and methods that will keep this software layer dynamic, contextually relevant, vital, and authentic? Where is the abstract and empathetic thinking you need to get there?

Why delegate offshore? Why bet your farm on generic Software as a Service tools that fail to differentiate you? Why dive head first into Big Data if abundant common sense data is big enough right now? Why get distracted by undifferentiated mobile apps or digital and social lipstick without working on the root cause, the genuine smile that comes from delivering an effortless customer experience? And finally, why fall victim to the IT versus Business trap (written requirements that lose everything in the translation) if you can now use abstract models and virtual story boards to generate all of the manual software code you need?

The first step is to think like a human again, galvanize your best businesspeople to focus on your customers, say no to manual coding and yes to computational thinking, and not get distracted by bright shiny technologies that are not completely aligned with your core values and strategies. Similarly, while difficult, it is equally important to leave your comfort zone of thinking inside-out. Inside-out software is not something you give to customers. Rather, it is dedicated to the worthy goal of automating silo back office business processes to eliminate waste, cycle time, and errors. While important for logistics, supply chain, human resources, and core operational efficiencies, these have become table stakes, rather than compelling differentiators.

What does an organization do when the majority of its technology investment is inside-out? It is obliged to put the burden of relevant customer engagement entirely on the shoulders of the chief marketing officer and customer service teams. These teams will use traditional branding, retail store design, advertising, and customer analytics for retention to wrap the organization's internal functions in ways they hope are attractive and appealing. But this is nothing more than very expensive window dressing. The empowered consumers Surowiecki writes about will see right through it.

Regardless of what kind of business you have, unless you learn how best to represent what is unique about your business, its authenticity, its promise, the collective strength of its culture, to a wider world using an immediately accessible software layer, you will continue to fall behind. Revenue and relevancy will steadily plummet in parallel.

The new software layer that will take you out of the twilight of the brands and into a dawn of continuous engagement must be *your* software. It must demonstrate your values, your commitment, and a deep and authentic empathy for your customers and how they interact with you. It must encompass nothing less than the best of your people, policies, and methods. And it must be good enough and strong enough that you can *give* it to your customers. It must be software personalized for your customers that adapts to each customer's context. Your customers will make it their own, use it to interact, and come to that point of trust at which they opt in to an always on, always learning, always adapting relationship with you. That means the software, like your relationships with your customers, will always be changing.

Once you get it right, this constant change will become your new normal. You will come to find it energizing. Stress will be replaced with the reward of knowing that with each moment of truth, you are earning and renewing customer trust and engagement. You are only as good as your next interaction or engagement. Static brand (fat, dumb, and deluded) has entered its twilight. Thanks to your software layer of engagement you share with your customers, a new always-on and always-adapting brand is emerging.

How much time do you have to realize this vision? That's not certain. The wisest choice is to start today.

NOTES

CHAPTER 1 CUSTOMERPOCALYPSE

1. Douglas Coupland, *Generation X: Tales for an Accelerated Culture*. (New York: St. Martin's Press, 1991).
2. William Strauss and Neil Howe, *Generations: The History of America's Future, 1584 to 2069*. (London: William Morrow & Co., 1991). See also Strauss and Howe, *Millennials Rising: The Next Great Generation*. (New York: Vintage, 2000).
3. Diane Theilfoldt and Devon Sheef, "Generation X and The Millennials: What You Need to Know About Mentoring the New Generations," *Law Practice Today*, November 2005, at www.americanbarorg.lpm/lpt/articles/mgt08044.html#author.
4. "Generation C: An Emerging Consumer Trend and Related New Business Ideas," *Trend Briefing*, February 2004, at www.trendwatching.com.
5. See, for example, Larry Weber, *Everywhere: Comprehensive Digital Business Strategy for the Social Media Era*. (Hoboken, NJ: John Wiley & Sons, 2011).
6. Michael B. Farrell, "E-mail Gets a Cold Shoulder," *Boston Globe*, March 29, 2013.
7. Craig Smith, "How Many People Use 378 of the Top Social Media, Apps & Services," *Digital Market Ramblings*, February 2014, at expandedramblings.com/index.php/resource-how-many-people-use-the-top-social-media/.
8. Alan L. Wurtzel, *Good to Great to Gone: The 60 Year Rise and Fall of Circuit City*. (New York: Diversion Publishing, 2012).
9. Louis Llovio, "Former Circuit City CEO and Chairman Talks of Company's Demise," *Richmond Times-Dispatch*, October 18, 2012, at www.timesdispatch.com/business/former-circuit-city-ceo-and-chairman-talks-of-company-s/article_8e219f23–721b-5a54-b6c2–3e1b35536557.html.
10. James Surowiecki, "Where Nokia Went Wrong," *The New Yorker* blog, September 3, 2013, at www.newyorker.com/online/blogs/currency/2013/09/where-nokia-went-wrong.html.
11. Rick Newman, "4 Lessons From the Demise of Borders," *U.S. News & World Report*, July 20, 2011, at www.usnews.com/news/blogs/rick-newman/2011/07/20/4-lessons-from-the-demise-of-borders.

12. Sam Gustin, "The Fatal Mistake That Doomed BlackBerry," *Time*, September 24, 2013, at http://business.time.com/2013/09/24/the-fatal-mistake-that-doomed-blackberry/.

13. George F. Colony and Peter Burris, "Technology Management in the Age of the Customer," Forrester Research, Inc., October 10, 2013.

14. Bruce Horovitz, "After Gen X, Millennials, What Should Next Generation Be?" *USA Today*, May 3, 2012, at usatoday30.usatoday.com/money/advertising/story/2012–05–03/naming-the-next-generation/54737518/1.

15. Dmitry Dragilev, "Xbox One, Netflix, Charles Schwab: Why Consumer Collaboration Is Key in Business," *Wired*, June 25, 2013, at www.wired.com/insights/2013/06/xbox-one-netflix-charles-schwab-why-consumer-collaboration-is-the-way-to-do-business-2/.

16. Don Mattrick, "Your Feedback Matters—Update on Xbox One," *Xbox Wire*, at news.xbox.com/2013/06/update.

17. Colony and Burris, "Technology Management."

18. "Nielsen: Global Consumers' Trust in 'Earned' Advertising Grows in Importance," April 10, 2012, at www.nielsen.com/us/en/press-room/2012/nielsen-global-consumers-trust-in-earned-advertising-grows.html.

19. Michael Maoz, "How Customer Service Drives Loyalty Through Customer Engagements," Gartner Research G00256977, October 16, 2013.

20. Focus Groups, Cambridge, MA, December 2013.

21. www.facebook.com/pages/United-Airlines-Sucks/216811830719.

22. www.youtube.com/watch?v=5YGc4zOqozo.

23. Dave Carroll, *United Breaks Guitars: The Power of One Voice in the Age of Social Media*. (Carlsbad, CA: Hays House, 2012).

24. Focus groups, Cambridge, MA, December 2013.

25. Focus groups.

26. Quoted in Kristine Ellis, "Lush," *Retail Merchandiser*, 2011, at www.retail-merchandiser.com/index.php/reports/retail-reports/94-lush-2.

27. Focus groups.

28. Focus groups.

29. Focus groups.

30. Focus groups.

31. Peter Burris, "Linking Customer Engagement to Business Capabilities in the Age of the Customer," Forrester Research, Inc., October 21, 2013.

CHAPTER 2 DEATH BY DATA

1. Christy Heady, "Gimmicky Banking Charges Keep Compounding," *The Chicago Tribune*, August 13, 1993, at articles.chicagotribune.com/1993–08–13/business/9308130060_1_live-teller-first-chicago-new-fees.

2. Sarah Gordon, "Ryanair Confirms It WILL Bring in Charges for On-Board Toilets," *The Daily Mail* (London), at www.dailymail.co.uk/travel/article-1263905/Ryanair-toilet-charges-phased-in.html#ixzz2NS8vjKEn.

3. Dmitry Dragilev, "Xbox One, Netflix, Charles Schwab: Why Consumer Collaboration Is Key in Business," *Wired*, June 25, 2013, at www.wired.com/insights/2013/06/xbox-one-netflix-charles-schwab-why-consumer-collaboration-is-the-way-to-do-business-2/.

4. John Markoff, "Double Helix Serves Double Duty," *New York Times*, January 28, 2013, at www.nytimes.com/2013/01/29/science/using-dna-to-store-digital-information.html?_r=0

5. "CRM Software Key Terms," at www.business.com/guides/crm-software-key-terms-34278.

6. Walter Isaacson, *Steve Jobs*. (New York: Simon & Schuster, 2011).

7. Mark Zuckerberg, "Our Commitment to the Facebook Community," November 29, 2011, at www.facebook.com/notes/facebook/our-commitment-to-the-facebook-community/10150378701937131.

8. Kashmir Hill, "How Target Figured Out a Teen Girl Was Pregnant Before Her Father Did," *Forbes*, February 16, 2012, at www.forbes.com/sites/kashmirhill/2012/02/16/how-target-figured-out-a-teen-girl-was-pregnant-before-her-father-did/.

9. Charles Duhigg, "How Companies Learn Your Secrets," *New York Times Sunday Magazine*, February 16, 2012, at www.nytimes.com/2012/02/19/magazine/shopping-habits.html?pagewanted=1&_r=2&hp.

CHAPTER 3   ADDING JUDGMENT AND DESIRE

1. Marc Beaujean, Jonathan Davidson, and Stacey Madge, "The 'Moment of Truth' in Customer Service," *McKinsey Quarterly*, February 2006, at www.mckinsey.com/insights/organization/the_moment_of_truth_in_customer_service.

2. Bertrand Russell, *The Scientific Outlook*. (New York: W.W. Norton & Co., 1931).

3. Penny Crosman, "PNC Builds a Real-Time Marketing Data Hub," *American Banker*, October 21, 2013, at www.americanbanker.com/issues/178_203/pnc-builds-a-real-time-marketing-data-hub-1063015-1.

4. The author wishes to acknowledge the assistance of PNC Bank for its review of this section of the book related to PNC Bank.

5. Peter Burris, "Business Capabilities in the Age of the Customer," Forrester Research, Inc., October 21, 2013.

6. Transforming Customer Service with Real-Time Predictive Analytics," *Pega's Build for Change Digest* podcast, July 27, 2012, at www.pega.com/resources/transforming-customer-service-with-real-time-predictive-analytics.

7. "Customer Loyalty in Retail Banking," Bain & Company, Global Edition 2012.

8. Garry Kasparov, "The Chess Master and the Computer," *The New York Review of Books*, February 11, 2010.

9. Hartosh Singh Bal, "Chessmate," *International Herald Tribune*, June 5, 2012.

CHAPTER 4 GETTING IT DONE WITH CUSTOMER PROCESSES

1. Steve Hawkes, "Tesco Has Lost the Plot, Say Stockbrokers—Neither Value nor Quality," *The Telegraph*, December 10, 2013, at blogs.telegraph.co.uk/news/stevehawkes/100250017/tesco-has-lost-the-plot-say-stockbrokers-neither-value-nor-quality/.

2. "Google Acquires Motorola Mobility," Google Investor Relations Press Release, May 22, 2012, at investor.google.com/releases/2012/0522.html.

3. Michael J. De La Merced, "Did Google Really Lose on Its Original Motorola Deal?" DealB%k Blog, *New York Times*, January 29, 2014, at dealbook.nytimes.com/2014/01/29/did-google-really-lose-on-its-original-motorola-deal/?_php=true&_type=blogs&smid=tw-dealbook&seid=auto&_r=0.

4. Peter Burris, "Business Capabilities in the Age of the Customer," Forrester Research, Inc., October 21, 2013.

5. "Credit Unions and PNC Deliver Best Customer Experience in Banking," *Customer Experience Matters* blog, February 23, 2012, at experiencematters.wordpress.com/?s=PNC.

6. Corporate Insight, "Online Marketing and Promotion," *Bank Monitor Report 2012*, January 2012.

7. Penny Crosman, "PNC Builds a Real-Time Marketing Data Hub," *American Banker*, October 21, 2013, at www.americanbanker.com/issues/178_203/pnc-builds-a-real-time-marketing-data-hub-1063015-1.

CHAPTER 5 CHANGE HOW YOU THINK ABOUT TECHNOLOGY

1. "Accenture Technology Vision 2013: Every Business Is a Digital Business," at www.accenture.com/us-en/technology/technology-labs/Pages/insight-technology-vision-2013.aspx.

2. Lisa Arthur, "Five Years from Now, CMOs Will Spend More on IT Than CIOs Do," *Forbes*, CMO Network, February 8, 2012, at www.forbes.com/sites/lisaarthur/2012/02/08/five-years-from-now-cmos-will-spend-more-on-it-than-cios-do/.

3. George F. Colony and Peter Burris, "Technology Management in the Age of the Customer," Forrester Research, Inc., October 10, 2013.

4. BBC, "'London Whale' Traders Charged in U.S. over $6.2bn Loss," August 14, 2013, at www.bbc.co.uk/news/business-23692109.
5. Chris Isidore and James O'Toole, "JPMorgan Fined $920 Million in 'London Whale' Trading Loss," CNN, September 19, 2013, at money.cnn .com/2013/09/19/investing/jpmorgan-london-whale-fine/.
6. Ellen Messmer, "Does 'Shadow IT' Lurk in Your Company?" *Network World*, August 8, 2012, at www.networkworld.com/news/2012/080812-shadow-it-261502.html.
7. Jill Dyche, "Shadow IT Is Out of the Closet," *Harvard Business Review*, HBR Blog Network, September 13, 2012, at blogs.hbr.org/cs/2012/09/shadow_it_is_out_of_the_closet.html.
8. See www.omg.org.
9. Symantec, "Avoiding the Hidden Costs of the Cloud," 2013, at www .symantec.com/content/en/us/about/media/pdfs/b-state-of-cloud-global-results-2013.en-us.pdf.
10. The manifesto comprises only a few lines of text and may be read at agilemanifesto.org.

CHAPTER 6   LIBERATING YOUR ORGANIZATION

1. Lee Fleming, "Perfecting Cross-Pollination," *Harvard Business Review*, September 2004.
2. Carole Rizzo, former chief information officer of Kaiser Permanente, speaking at PegaWORLD 2008, Washington, DC.
3. "Telstra Takes Aim at the 'Wow Factor' with Its Customer Centric Approach," *Pega's Build for Change Digest* podcast, December 4, 2013, at www.pega.com/resources/telstra-takes-aim-at-the-wow-factor-with-its-customer-centric-approach.
4. Harley Manning and Kerry Bodine, *Outside In: The Power of Putting Customers at the Center of Your Business*. (Boston: New Harvest, 2012).
5. At www.businessdictionary.com/definition/customer-service.html.
6. At www.investopedia.com/terms/c/customer-service.asp#axzz2IvkyuY4e.
7. Efraim Turban, David King, Jae Lee, Merrill Warkentin, H. Michael Chung, and Michael Chung, *Electronic Commerce 2002: A Managerial Perspective*, 2nd ed. (Upper Saddle River, NJ: Prentice-Hall, 2002).
8. Jack Speer, "What Is the Definition of Customer Service?" *BizWatch Online*, at www.bizwatchonline.com/BWJuly06/article3_0904.htm.
9. Fred Reichheld (with Rob Markey), *The Ultimate Question 2.0: How Net Promoter Companies Thrive in a Customer-Driven World*. (Boston: Harvard Business Review Press, 2011).

10. Janette Sadik-Khan, "The Benefits of a Well-Designed City," *Bloomberg Businessweek*, January 24, 2013, at www.businessweek.com/articles/2013–01–24/ janette-sadik-khan-the-benefits-of-a-well-designed-city.

11. Peter Burris, "Business Capabilities in the Age of the Customer," Forrester Research, Inc., October 21, 2013.

CHAPTER 7 YOU ARE YOUR SOFTWARE— THE DIGITAL IMPERATIVE

1. www.frankbyocbc.com.

2. Peter Dahlström and David Edelman, "The Coming Era of 'On-Demand' Marketing," *McKinsey Quarterly*, April 2013.

3. Penny Crosman, "PNC Builds a Real-Time Marketing Data Hub," *American Banker*, October 21, 2013, at www.americanbanker.com/issues/178_203/ pnc-builds-a-real-time-marketing-data-hub-1063015–1.

4. Thomas Wailgum, "You Say IT, Forrester Says BT: What's the Difference?" *CIO*, September 24, 2009, at www.cio.com/article/503221/ You_Say_IT_Forrester_Says_BT_What_s_the_Difference_.

5. Peter Burris, "The CIO Mandate: Engaging Customers with Business Technology," Forrester Research, Inc., November 15, 2013.

6. "The Digital Customer: It's Time to Play to Win and Stop Playing Not to Lose," Accenture, at www.accenture.com/us-en/Pages/insight-digital-customer-play-to-win-summary.aspx.

7. "Accenture 2013 Global Consumer Pulse Survey," Executive Summary, at www.accenture.com/SiteCollectionDocuments/PDF/Accenture-Global-Consumer-Pulse-Research-Study-2013-Key-Findings.pdf.

8. Accenture, "The Digital Customer."

9. Nicholas Carr, *The Big Switch: Rewiring the World, from Edison to Google*. (New York: W.W. Norton & Company, 2008).

10. Marc Andreessen, "Why Software Is Eating the World," *Wall Street Journal*, August 20, 2011, at http://online.wsj.com/news/articles/SB100014240531119 03480904576512250915629460.

11. Michael Maoz, "What Every CIO Could Learn From Tufts University About Understanding the Customer Experience," March 19, 2014, at blogs.gartner .com/michael_maoz.

12. George F. Colony and Peter Burris, "Technology Management in the Age of the Customer," Forrester Research, Inc., October 10, 2013.

13. Accenture, "The Digital Customer."

14. James Surowiecki, "Twilight of the Brands," *New Yorker*, February 17, 2014, at www.newyorker.com/talk/financial/2014/02/17/140217ta_talk_surowiecki.

15. Jeannette M. Wing, "Computational Thinking," *Communications of the ACM* 49, no. 3 (2006): 33–35.

INDEX